Interpreting Interviews

SAGE has been part of the global academic community since 1965, supporting high quality research and learning that transforms society and our understanding of individuals, groups, and cultures. SAGE is the independent, innovative, natural home for authors, editors and societies who share our commitment and passion for the social sciences.

Find out more at: **www.sagepublications.com**

Interpreting Interviews

Mats Alvesson

SAGE

Los Angeles | London | New Delhi
Singapore | Washington DC

© Mats Alvesson 2011

First published 2011

SAGE Publications Ltd
1 Oliver's Yard
55 City Road
London EC1Y 1SP

SAGE Publications Inc.
2455 Teller Road
Thousand Oaks, California 91320

SAGE Publications India Pvt Ltd
B 1/I 1 Mohan Cooperative Industrial Area
Mathura Road
New Delhi 110 044

SAGE Publications Asia-Pacific Pte Ltd
33 Pekin Street #02-01
Far East Square
Singapore 048763

Library of Congress Control Number: 2010931399

British Library Cataloguing in Publication data

A catalogue record for this book is available from
the British Library

ISBN 978-0-85702-257-8
ISBN 978-0-85702-258-5 (pbk)

Typeset by C&M Digitals (P) Ltd, Chennai, India
Printed in India at Replika Press Pvt Ltd
Printed on paper from sustainable resources.

CONTENTS

PREFACE

In contemporary Western society, interviews are routinely carried out as a way of gaining knowledge about all kinds of phenomena. This society can – with some justice – be referred to as an interview society. It is easy to accept the interview as a good and economical way to learn about things, but then it is also easy to underestimate the problem of relying on responses to questions as valid sources of information. Much has been written on methods, but much still remains to be said. In particular there is a bias towards technical and practical issues, while the more intellectual side of interviews tends to be downplayed. This book shows how this proves highly problematic and it develops a framework for thinking about the research interview. Dominating neo-positivist and romantic views on the interview are criticized. Following conversational and discourse analysts as well as other critics, the capacity of the interview to function as a pipeline for the transmission of experience and meaning to the researcher is questioned. Eight metaphors offering reconceptualizations of the interview are suggested, drawing upon recent theoretical trends in language, the individual (subject) and discourse. A reflexive theoretical framework is developed. The book suggests new ways of dealing with interviews with implications for fieldwork, the interaction with subjects, the interpretation of empirical material and potential or suitable research questions to be addressed based on interviews.

This book draws upon a paper published in *Academy of Management Review* 1: 2003 and to some extent also on a variety of empirical and methodological projects of mine during a couple of decades. My ambition has been, and remains, to cover the most vital aspects of qualitative research from a non-technical, reflexive point of view. An overall framework was published in *Reflexive Methodology*, (Sage, 2nd edition, 2009, with Kaj Sköldberg). The present book is to some extent an application of a general reflexive approach to the research interview.

I am grateful to Kiren Shoman at SAGE for encouraging me to write this book. I am also grateful to the anonymous reviewers consulted by SAGE as well as Jacqueline Colleary and Stefan Sveningsson, Lund University, Yvonne Billing, University of Copenhagen and Eero Vara, Swedish School of Economics, Helsinki, who commented on a draft of the book manuscript.

Lund, December 2009
Mats Alvesson

1

INTRODUCTION

Social science is fairly strongly oriented towards empirical research in the form of getting knowledge out of subjects by asking them to provide it, whether they are answering interview questions, filling in questionnaires or writing diaries. There is a strong belief that the 'collection' and processing of data can provide a solid base for saying yes or no to various hypotheses and theories. Alternatively, as in grounded theory, the data are presumed to guide researchers to understand specific phenomena and develop theory. This great faith in data and empirical inquiry as a cornerstone in knowledge development has been challenged by a multitude of intellectual streams during recent years. These range from interpretivist approaches emphasizing the centrality of pre-understandings, paradigms and metaphors in research work, to poststructuralists, discursivists and constructivists denying science any privileged access to the objective truth about the social world (Steier, 1991). Interpretivists emphasize that there are no facts, only interpretations which depend on meanings ascribed by the interpreter. Language-focused scholars view discourse as central and argue that language constructs rather than mirrors phenomena. This makes representation and thus empirical work privileging 'data' a basically problematic enterprise (Alvesson & Kärreman, 2000a; Gergen & Gergen, 1991). When researchers interact with subjects – undertaking interviews, making observations, requiring responses to questionnaires – they are not just revealing the truth about social conditions and people's experiences through accessing data, they are also producing specific representations of something. These representations are then sometimes naively taken for granted as mirrors of 'reality'. (For broad reviews of the problems of mirroring or capturing reality, see e.g. Alvesson & Sköldberg, 2009; Denzin & Lincoln, 1994; Van Maanen, 1995.)

The critique of positivism and neopositivism, including many versions of qualitative research, type grounded theory, has been massive over the years, but this has not prevented the majority of researchers from doing normal science more or less as if nothing had happened. Questionnaire researchers still assume that the X's put in small squares by respondents make it possible to determine what goes on in the social world. Qualitative researchers still present interview statements as if they were pathways to the interiors of those being interviewed or mirrors of social practice. Although it is broadly recognized that data need to be interpreted in order to say anything and that all data are fused with theory, data are still seen as a basic building bloc and an arbitrator of truth (valid knowledge) in much social science. To collect and sort (codify) interview statements is a trusted and robust ground for qualitative research. One problem with the critique of the capacity of social science to deliver empirically grounded knowledge is that it is rather absolutist, is perceived as destructive and is therefore neglected. Another problem is that much of this critique addresses philosophical and epistemological issues, while research practices have received much less attention. The latter are largely viewed – in most method texts as well as in research reports – as technical or practical matters, separated from wider theoretical and philosophical ideas about knowledge production. Method (ideas on how to produce and make sense of empirical material) still largely remains comparatively unaffected by all the theoretical and philosophical work that has tremendous relevance for our understanding of methodological practices. The wealth of insights about problems of developing knowledge and the limitations of social science as a rational project need to be connected to research practices and used to inspire and revise these. It seems vital to make a stronger link between more philosophically inclined discussions and practical and technical method issues. This is the context and overall ambition with the present book.

This book addresses qualitative interviewing, although many of the themes have a broad relevance for social and behavioural research in general. Qualitative research has become increasingly common in social studies. This is often exclusively or mainly based on interviews. The focus of this book is primarily interviews aiming to get 'rich accounts', i.e. normally relatively loosely structured interviews with face-to-face contact. They are typically relatively time-consuming to carry out and can lead to varied responses from interviewees. Qualitative interviews – in opposition to highly structured 'talking questionnaires' (Potter and Wetherell, 1987) – are fairly open to what the interviewee feels is relevant and important to talk about, given the interests of the research project. Advocates of interviews would typically argue that this approach is beneficial in as much as a rich account of interviewees' experiences, knowledge, ideas and impressions may be considered and documented (Bryman et al., 1988; Fontana and Frey, 1994, 2005; Holstein & Gubrium, 1997).

For a long time, and to a degree still around today, researchers doing this kind of interviewing suffered attacks from advocates of what was considered to be more rigorous methods. This view often implies that there should be some kind of formal instrument between researcher and subjects, presumably leading to rationality, transparency and control. Here the experiment was seen to be optimal, but questionnaires and structured interviews were also deemed acceptable. Quantification is another part of this rigour idea, as this is supposed to reduce arbitrariness in the data processing work, and to involve a reliable process and the subsequent delivery of clear and robust results, with not very much depending on the subjectivity of the researcher. The critique from quantitative research has lost some of its force over the years, at least in most fields, partly as the result of an even harsher critique of the alternatives to qualitative research and, more generally, of positivism. Advocates of qualitative research, including interviews, have with some success argued for the benefits of more flexible approaches, making it possible to take the experiences and observations of those studied seriously into account and thus get richer description and the inspiration for new ideas.

Conventional views of qualitative research, including interview-based studies, have however faced other critics who would question the basic assumptions of interviews being about the expression and transformation of knowledge from people out there to the researcher. There is increased recognition that while we live in an 'interview society' where interviews in the mass media, entertainment and other contexts are routinely carried out so that most people are accustomed to this form and practice, gathering and exhibiting such knowledge is not as straightforward as it seems (Dingwall, 1997; Silverman, 2006). Interview talk may say more about role-playing and adapting to social standards in the name of impression management – including how to appear authentic – than about how people really feel or what social reality is really like. It is not evident that even ambitious social scientists can score much better than Dr Phil or Oprah Winfrey in providing the

3

public with good knowledge about people's lives. Critics also raise concerns about the sloppiness of interview standards: 'Interviews are carried out time and again with little hesitation and hardly an afterthought. The individual interview has become a ubiquitous feature of everyday life' (Holstein & Gubrium, 2003a: 4). Some people believe that the interview method is over-used in social science. Kvale (1996) talks of a flight from statistics and think that some people prefer interviews because these are seen as an easy option. Dingwall (1997) sees this flight rather as being from observational and ethnographic studies, reflecting a desire to do quick and dirty research and thus avoid the more demanding empirical work of 'being there' for a longer period.

Understanding interviews as a superior technique for tapping knowing subjects for knowledge about their experiences and/or social practices neglects the interview situation as a socially and linguistically complex situation, critics argue. Interview accounts may just as well be seen as the outcomes of political considerations, script-following, impression management, the operation of discourses constituting subjects and governing their responses – to mention just a few of the themes I will address in this book. Arguably, these are key features of social and organizational life. But most research reports seem to assume that these are absent from or can be minimized in the interview situation, or that the good researcher can somehow bypass or abstract from these. It is important not to simplify and idealize the interview situation, not to assume that the interviewee is primarily a competent and moral truth teller, acting in the service of science, producing the data needed to reveal the 'interiors' of the interviewees (experiences, feelings, values) or the practices of social institutions. It is also important not to see social and linguistic complexities as merely sources of bias. My argument is that the interview, as a complex social event, calls for a theoretical understanding, or rather a reflexive approach in which a set of various theoretical viewpoints can be considered and, when there are reasons for doing so, applied. Without a theoretical understanding supporting our critical judgment, any use of interview material risks naivety and leaves interpretations standing on shaky ground.

It is also important to be aware of the limited range of what can be captured through interviews. Things happen outside of that which is directly registered by individuals and focused on by researchers. Many researchers will distance themselves from the methodological individualism (a focus on the actor level) favoured by most qualitative researchers, especially those relying on interviews. Critical realists, for example, would argue that 'actors' accounts are both corrigible and limited by the existence of unacknowledged conditions, unintended consequences, tacit skills and unconscious motivations' (Bhaskar, 1998: xvi). Learning through talking with people is marginalized if not dismissed by Archer through a reference to broader and deeper elements of society: 'we do not uncover real structures by interviewing people in-depth about them' (1998: 199). However, any alternatives to such uncovering activities – the use of statistics, questionnaires, experiments, observations, textual analysis – may not score any better, at least not with regard to indicating the 'real structures'. Nevertheless it is important to think also about what may go on outside of an interviewee's experiences and worldview.

The present book takes the possibilities, problems and limitations of interviews seriously, advocating what I will refer to as a reflexivity approach to interview research. This means that I think we should avoid giving interview material an a priori status (as indicative of reality or meanings) and instead think through a set of interpretive possibilities for assessing what the material is about and for what purposes it can be used. A willingness to challenge and revise one's initial position is vital here. This thinking through and possible position-revision calls for strong theoretical support. This book aims to provide it.

Purpose and structure of the book

The book is an effort to connect a 'high-brow' methodology – including meta-theoretical issues – with a 'low-brow' method – field practices – as well as with social theory. I attempt to consider philosophical traditions like critical theory and poststructuralism, as well as the practice of doing interviews. As a social event, the interview calls for theory to be understood. Empiricism, common sense, good intentions and a (in most cases deceptive) belief in one's own openness and interpersonal ability as an interviewer are not enough. Being an experienced interview researcher is no guarantee for possessing the ability to control an interview and produce good research results. An impression that one's interviewees are trustworthy is too loose a basis for doing social research.

The *first* aim of the book is thus to review and develop a broad critique of dominant understandings of the interview in social research,

5

indicating substantive problems with using interviews to tap interviewees for knowledge of their social realities and/or their subjective worlds. The *second* aim is to suggest utilizing interviews in ways that are more theoretically well-informed. I propose methodological guidelines for a more reflexive approach to qualitative research. This offers a better balance between options and problems in the interview than seems to be common. The upside of interviews – options and potentials – is typically emphasized, while limits and shortcomings are neglected or marginalized. We need to fully consider both sets of aspects. The guidelines, in particular, not only have a bearing on the interpretation and use of interview material, but also for interview practices and the research questions we can ask in the context of interview-based studies. The *third* aim, implicit in the first and second, is to suggest some ideas for a theory or rather a meta-theory of the research interview. Theory is used in a loose and unconventional sense, indicating a framework and set of concepts for thinking about the subject matter, asking questions and encouraging thinking that breaks with common sense. In this context theory is coupled to methodology and is not aimed at giving an explanation of interview behaviour as an objective in itself, it is more related to how we can understand it in a sophisticated way and then have a good idea of what to do with interview accounts. An important aspect here is the metaphor adopted for the interview situation and interview accounts. A metaphor can provide an image or a gestalt offering a specific view of the subject. Through comparing the interview situation with something else and perhaps unexpected, we understand it in a different and perhaps more imaginative way than as a tool for data collection. Drawing attention to metaphors encourages a re-conceptualization of the interview which involves theoretical abstraction and the use of a vocabulary that also encourages an openness to complex patterns and depth thinking, thus moving beyond a view of interviews as the optimization of techniques and the minimization of bias.

Taken together the three aims mean that an alternative strategy for using interview material is proposed. It suggests that we look upon interviews and interview outcomes as existing in a field of tensions between different forces and logics. A *reflexive pragmatism* view on the interview is proposed. A key element here is to acknowledge as fully as possible the complexity and uncertainty of the research practice and to realize that any meaning pulled out of interviews for example is contestable. Careful consideration of how interview texts can be interpreted and used is necessary. This approach means working with alternative lines of interpretation and vocabularies and reinterpreting the favoured line(s) of understanding through the systematic drawing upon any alternative points of departure (Alvesson & Sköldberg, 2009). Perspective-shifting is thus central. Reflexivity operates with a metatheoretical structure that guides an interplay between producing interpretations and challenging them. Reflexivity includes opening up the phenomena through exploring more than one set of meanings and acknowledging ambiguity in the phenomena addressed and the line(s) of inquiry favoured. *Reflexivity* means a bridging of the gap between epistemological concerns and method. *Pragmatism* means a balancing of endless reflexivity and radical scepticism with a sense of direction and a commitment to accomplishing a result. Pragmatism also includes considerations of relevance and means a bracketing of uncertainty and indecisiveness in favour of a wish to offer some good interpretations and to try to encourage understanding of a well-picked topic of inquiry. This approach means that interviews are potentially valuable for making 'strong' knowledge claims, but only after careful consideration and perhaps often in more modest ways than seem to be common.

The purpose with all this is not (primarily) to make life difficult for the interviewer – even though adding complexity does not make existence any simpler. The purpose is partly to encourage critical consciousness of the problems of interviewing, partly to suggest new and more imaginative ways of thinking and doing of interviews. Hopefully, this can contribute to less naive and more thought through, and more creative interview-based studies. This calls for some challenging of the technical focus and the great faith in sorting and categorizing interview responses (seen as indicators of some 'truth' outside the interview situation).

The book is structured as follows. The next chapter reviews predominant perspectives on the interview in social science studies. Three such perspectives are highlighted and labelled as neo-positivism, romanticism and localism. Chapter 3 fairly briefly addresses some practical issues in interviews. Chapter 4 addresses the concept of metaphor and argues for taking metaphors (or images) for interviews seriously. Do we, for example, see the interview as an instrument for information gathering or as a setting for the exercise of conversational skills? The two views reflect different understandings of what the interview is about, as highlighted by two quite different metaphors – instrument and conversation. The significance and value of taking the metaphorical level seriously for getting a deeper and more imaginative

7

understanding of interviews are underscored. Chapter 5 then presents eight alternative conceptualizations of what the research interview is about, summarized in terms of metaphors. Each of these offers a critique of mainstream ideas on interviews and suggests paths for using interview material in different and often unconventional ways. Chapter 6 addresses ways of using the set of alternative metaphors in a systematic and integrated way. Here the concept of reflexivity is central, drawing attention to how various metaphors can be used to confront and challenge various understandings and to force the researcher to think through a range of analytical options and possible interpretive routes before deciding how to use interview material. In Chapter 7, some of the possible implications of this view are outlined. These concern: a) implications for methodological practice and technique; b) implications for a more rigorous and reflexive approach to using interview material for 'conventional' purposes; c) implications for novel research questions and new lines of interpretation; and d) considerations about whether or not one should maintain empirical claims or downplay these, viewing empirical material as a source of inspiration for thinking and theory-development rather than for grounded description. These possible implications address reflexivity both as a way to increase rigour (by avoiding using interview data without thinking through what they are really 'worth' and being careful about overusing them) and/or imagination (by using the material for other and more unexpected purposes than the conventional ones). In the final chapter, the core arguments and ideas are summarized, the ethics of interpreting interviews are discussed, some conclusions are made and further food for thought is suggested.

2

VIEWS ON INTERVIEWS:
A SKEPTICAL REVIEW

As with all efforts to produce an overview of a research field, it is not obvious how to identify and label the main positions taken on interviews. All distinctions and divisions mean the arbitrary creation of order and patterns. It is common however to divide up the field as follows:

- *Structure* Interviews are divided up in terms of structured, semi-structured and unstructured. Structure is mainly a matter of degree. At one end we have the highly structured interview, where the entire process should run according to a clear plan and the delivery of interview statements should follow this neatly. At the other extreme we find almost entirely un-structured talks, where a broad theme is targeted and the researcher is open to the interview taking unexpected turns. The interviewee is free to partly define and develop the relevant sub-themes or issues, but the interviewer presumably wants to avoid too wide departures from the overall theme of the research project. In most cases, unstructured interviews are best described as loosely structured, where some questions are prepared and asked and various themes are to be covered, even if the interviewer may be fairly free and flexible also in this regard, perhaps being also inclined to follow departures from the initial area of interest.
- *Size* The size issue typically involves a choice between the single interviewee and a group of people, although interviews with pairs (e.g. couples) is a third option in some kinds of research. Within the overall area of group interviews there are different versions – from brainstorming groups with little or no structure, to highly structured settings like focus consumer groups in marketing and delphi groups where experts are tapped for their skills in forecasting, exploration and pretesting.
- *Communication media* The meeting form (media) of interviews varies respectively between face-to-face, telephonic or electronic. The majority of the interviews of interest for qualitative research will be face-to-face.

Telephonic and electronic interviews are seen as much poorer and not relevant in most cases where complex phenomena are being investigated, but are economical and can perhaps sometimes also be used for brief follow-up interviews in research aiming for 'richer' interview material.

- *Category* Various groups of people are sometimes believed to call for particular considerations in terms of interview methods. Indeed, there are texts on how to interview children, old people, elites, ethnic minorities, the culturally diverse, men and women (Holstein & Gubrium, 2003b). In particular, interviews with women have attained considerable interest from feminists with attention being paid to issues surrounding power relations, ethics and the exploitation of experiences in the relationship between a researcher and the persons being studied (Olesen, 2000; Reinharz & Chase, 2003). Some would point at dominant forms of language use as being potentially problematic in relationship to certain social groups. DeVault (1990: 96), for example, has argued that 'language itself reflects male experience, and that its categories are often incongruent with women's lives'. She exemplifies the terms 'work' and 'leisure' as being out of tune with the household and family work which, to a large extent, characterize the lives of females.

Overlapping the issue of category and the need to consider specific circumstances is the nature of the theme being studied. In particular, when interviews address very personal and very sensitive issues like those of sickness and death, family violence, sexual abuse, discrimination, and so on, certain considerations are called for.

Choices and ideas around the type and purpose of interviewing and the nature of topics addressed are of course important in research, but this book does not concentrate on technical and design issues and also, on the whole, refrains from dealing with the psychology involved in interviews about personally sensitive issues. I will only to a limited degree address these, mainly in Chapter 3. The contribution of this book is, as said previously, less on the psychological, practical or tactical aspects of doing interviews than on how we can work with theoretical ideas in order to better understand interviews and interpret the material coming out of these.

In the social and behavioural sciences there are, of course, different ways of providing overviews of more theoretical aspects of interviews. To some extent one can relate to basic paradigmatic positions, but there is no one-to-one relationship between, for example, a view on the very nature of society (e.g. whether this is characterized by class-conflict, pluralism or consensus/community) and interviews. Review authors will sometimes structure the field on epistemological grounds; sometimes they can provide overviews based on the interview purpose and design.

Other times they combine principles or dimensions for structuring. Fontana and Frey (2005) start with going through structured interviewing, group interviewing and unstructured interviewing and then they follow these with brief overviews of postmodern and gendered interviewing. The latter represent special, high-profiled foci within interview research.

Silverman (2006) identifies three major theoretical and epistemological positions on interviews: positivism, emotionalism and constructionism.[1] These focus respectively on facts, authentic experiences (personal meanings) and the construction of interview responses (talk). I will mainly follow, but also revise, this approach by using other concepts and defining them somewhat differently. Of course there is much variety in the field and it is difficult to represent all the different approaches. There is a trade-off between simplification and acknowledging complexity and variation. In order to hit a better balance between these considerations I will also address a middle position that I refer to as interactive rationalism.[2] The positions discussed are not entirely limited to interviews but do offer distinct views on these and I am concentrating on this method/research practice here.

Major positions taken to interviewing: neo-positivism, romanticism and localism

Neo-positivism

A traditional, and still today dominating, position is that of *neo-positivism*. I prefer 'neo' here as very few researchers choose to stick to the original meaning(s) of positivism with many relating rather loosely to tradition. Advocates are eager to establish a context-free truth about what is really 'out there' by following a research protocol and gathering responses relevant to it, minimizing researcher influence and other sources of 'bias'. There is an interest in 'facts' – about behaviours, practices, attitudes, values or whatever. It is viewed as vital to gain non-distorted data that can be compared or aggregated. It is therefore important that the data are not strongly affected by highly local circumstances such as the specifics of interview contexts. An interview will typically be carefully planned and tightly structured. If, for example, men and women are interviewed about childcare, political sympathies or television habits, the use of different questions or interaction styles with different interviewees would make it very difficult to know if any possible differences between men and women could be related to gender per se, or to differences in the interview situation where perhaps men and women are being interviewed in different ways. Guidelines for a good interview often involve issues such as:

- Not becoming involved in explanations of the study, being brief and using a standardized presentation.
- Not deviating from the structure of the interview.
- Being neutral and avoiding getting personal.

Of course, few would doubt some degree of interviewer effect or other contingencies influencing the outcome, but for the neo-positivists these are to be minimized. Here, 'the interview conversation is a pipeline for transmitting knowledge' (Holstein & Gubrium, 1997: 113). Interview questions 'are intended to tap individual experience' (Charmaz, 2003: 315). Even though it is typically recognized that emphatic sensitivity and judgment are necessary and the interview cannot be conducted mechanically, this is still mainly done following the stimuli-response format. Most interview-based research that is published in disciplines and journals dominated by conventional research standards tends to be neo-positivist. Researchers imitate quantitative ideals for data production, analysis and writing. Rules, procedures, an avoidance of bias, detailed coding, large quantities of material, and so on are emphasized in methodological texts as well as in empirical writings (e.g. Charmaz, 2003; Eisenhardt, 1989; Glaser & Strauss, 1967). The ideal is viewed as a completely transparent research process, characterized by objectivity and neutrality. It is seen as vital that the researcher can clearly describe what has been done and how and that the reader should then be able to assess the work. This calls for a minimization of variation and complexity in interview work.

Revised neo-positivism: interactive rationalism

The problem with this, as is being increasingly recognized, is that respondents may produce only superficial and cautious responses. Many researchers are aware of problems of trust and limited control over interviewee responses. In addition, the meaning of words used is often unclear – trying to understand meaning often calls for follow-up questions, which can sometimes create additional ambiguity as people are often incoherent in their talk (Potter & Wetherell, 1987). This reflects a more social and linguistic understanding of the situation.

As a result of this, researchers have developed techniques such as repeat interviews in order to establish better contact, checking for consistency over time/between situations and/or giving interviewees as well as interviewers a chance to reflect upon what has been said before (e.g. Acker et al., 1991; Charmaz, 2003; Collinson, 1992). Covaleski et al. (1998: 305) reported a large apparatus of various techniques to master the situation, some of which were intended to contribute to their efforts to 'move beyond the facade of the firms and "party-line" descriptions'. Success here meant that what the researchers saw as initial misleading accounts in interviews were abandoned in subsequent interviews. This approach can be said to offer a moderate breach with neo-positivism, and may be labelled *interactive rationalism*. It is assumed that confidence and depth call for a fairly close interaction. It is important for a researcher to get good access to a setting, understand the language and culture of respondents, think through how to present themself and the purpose of the study, perhaps find an informant (an insider who can be helpful in guiding that researcher into the setting studied), gaining trust, establishing a rapport, etc. (Fontana & Frey, 2005). Still, this is accomplished mainly around – rather than in – interviewing, which means that an interview can be carried out in a fairly neutral manner, without social interaction leading to bias within it. Interview statements are, on the whole, seen as valid data, or at least they are presented as if this were the case.

Interactive rationalism to some extent recognizes social complexity and embraces 'soft' and flexible technical measures in dealing with the problem of how to maximize reliable responses. Techniques include continually sharing any emerging interpretations and insights with those studied, conducting interviews of various kinds and in various places (e.g. offices, homes, cafés), returning transcripts of life histories to interviewees for their feedback, performing extensive member checks by sharing interpretations with participants, talking at length with key informants, etc. (Covaleski et al., 1998: 305ff). This position tends to share with neo-positivism the assumption that interview responses at the end of the day accurately reflect the experiences and/or observations of interviewees.

Romanticism

A second view on interviews can be called *romanticism*. By this, Dingwall (1997) means that the nearer we come to the respondent, the closer we are to apprehending the real self. Through closeness and depth we can find the authentic and true, which are simply being expressed in our talk. Silverman (2006), while also referring to romanticism, talks about 'emotionalism', where the data should be about authentic subjective experiences which are revealed through unstructured, open-ended interviews. I prefer romanticism, as the theme of what is being addressed is not only or necessarily emotions but also ideas, values, understandings of practices, efforts to reconstruct processes and interactions, and so on may be targeted as well. Interest lies in getting rich accounts and the open interview is a way to produce these.

The romantic researcher, advocating a more 'genuine' human interaction, believes in establishing a rapport, trust and commitment between interviewer and interviewee, thus turning the interview into a 'warm' situation. Here the interviewee is free to express him or herself authentically and will produce open, rich and trustworthy talk. These are a prerequisite in order to be able to explore the inner world (meanings, ideas, feelings, intentions) or experienced social reality of the interviewee. The typical ambition of interview-studies is to accomplish 'deeper, fuller conceptualisations of those aspects of our subjects' lives we are most interested in understanding' (Miller & Glassner, 1997: 103). Researchers will rely on interviewees' narrations about their lives as a way to understand them, as 'story-telling stays closer to actual life-events than methods that elicit explanations' (Hollway & Jefferson, 2000: 32).

Romantics emphasize an interactivity with and closeness to interviewees more than interactive rationalists. Romantics take seriously the risk that interviewees are guided by expectations of what the researcher wants to hear and social norms for how a person should express themself. They also believe, however, that establishing close personal contact with respondents – who are then seen as 'participants' instead – may minimize this problem. Fontana and Frey (1994), for example, suggested that a researcher may reject 'outdated' techniques of avoiding getting involved or providing a personal opinion and instead engage in a 'real' conversation with 'give and take' and 'emphatic understanding':

> This makes the interview more honest, morally sound, and reliable, because it treats the respondent as an equal, allows him or her to express personal feelings, and therefore presents a more 'realistic' picture that can be uncovered using traditional interview methods. (1994: 371)

An emphasis on empathy and the development of trust are assumed to solve the problem. Other advocates of interviews talk about 'active interviewing' as an ideal form (Ellis et al., 1997; Holstein & Gubrium, 1997, 2003a). Here, the idea is that a researcher's interventions can transform the interview subject 'from a repository of opinions and reasons or a wellspring of emotions into a productive source of knowledge' (Holstein & Gubrium, 1997: 121), as 'the subject's interpretative capabilities must be activated, stimulated and cultivated' (p. 122). The interview subject has potentially much of value to say, but this calls for the researcher to actively lead or support that subject into intelligent talk. Interviewer and interviewee thus collaborate in the 'co-construction of knowledge'. The positions of the two then become less distinct and the value of the terms may in some cases be questionable.

One could say that some interview proponents have responded to the critique of the more cool, minimalistic versions of interviewing – aiming to avoid bias – by advocating *hyper-romanticism*, i.e. escalating efforts to accomplish 'depth' and authenticity by turning the interview into a moral peak performance (as in the quotation from Fontana and Frey above), or by utilizing activism through turning the interviewee into a focused and systematic knowledge producer (as exemplified by Holstein and Gubrium).[3] Some authors, in rejecting the passive interviewer and interviewee, go so far as to celebrate the empowerment of interviewees, the becoming of 'participants', who together with the researcher engage in a collective project of knowledge development. In this 'team effort', the enterprise 'works against asymmetry, emphasizing a more fundamental sense of the shared task at hand, which now becomes a form of "collaboration" in the production of meaning' (Holstein & Gubrium, 2003a: 19).

Some feminist work also fits with this label when seeing the good interview as one guided by feminist values like the minimization of power differences, empathy, care, sensitivity and other good things, providing 'a great spectrum of responses and a greater insight into the lives of the respondents' or participants (Fontana & Frey, 2005: 711). According to Denzin (1997: 275) 'the feminist, communitarian researcher does not invade the privacy of others, use informed consent forms, select subjects randomly, or measure research designs in terms of their validity. This framework presumes a scholar who builds collaborative, reciprocal, trusting and friendly relationships with those studied ...'. Some feminists are sceptical about overly excessive assumptions and ambitions. Reinharz and Chase (2003: 81) for example, raise doubts regarding the 'romanticization of the woman-to-woman interview' developing 'sisterly bonds', which is perhaps more frequently expressed in earlier feminist work. At the same time, most feminists share at least a moderate version of a romantic research view ('romanticism light'), while it seems to be becoming increasingly common to acknowledge some of complexities involved in the relationship between interviewer and interviewee.

An interesting deviation from the idea that closeness, empathy and expressed understanding will create conditions for the good interview is that of Schwalbe and Wolkomir (2003), who in discussing interviewing men believe that their inclination, in a patriarchical society, to protect a certain sense of self and image will mean that they are reluctant to open up. This calls for various tricks and tactics in order to outflank men's defence barriers, including a desire to control the interview and to put up a façade of being rational and strong, thereby making it difficult for the interviewer to reach deeper and more authentic material. This approach shares with the romantics the conviction that an active and flexible interviewer can access some kind of truth, given a sensitive reading and handling of the interaction and the interviewee's responses.

Although the various forms of 'warm' interviewing sound sympathetic (even if 'interviewing men' could be seen as involving some manipulation), they hardly, as Fontana and Frey (1994) indicated, guarantee 'truthful' interview statements that give a 'realistic' picture. They may lead to interview outcomes that are strongly tied to the idiosyncrasies of the situation and moves by the interviewer affecting the mind state and responses of the interviewee in unpredictable ways.

Ambitious interviewers will often emphasize the ideal of establishing a familiarity, dialogue and relationship *vis-à-vis* research respondents, perhaps performing repeat interviews in order to build on this further and to be able to evaluate accounts for their consistency over time (see for example Collinson, 1992). Such ideals are important, but they only help to solve the problem to a limited extent, namely that accounts are characterized by the social situation in which they are produced, the imperfections of language in their descriptions and transmissions of meaning, and the fact that they tend to vary not only from one telling to another but even within a set of utterances produced on one particular occasion. What interviewers can attain at best – if they want to describe something beyond language use – is utterances that are 'more or less' consistent across different interviews and occasions. But if we pay serious attention to the ideas of discourse analysis, studying in detail how people talk (Potter & Wetherell, 1987) and how this varies with context, then we would probably expect return interviews to lead to variations in accounts.

In Acker et al. (1991) a case is described that involved four repeat interviews. The content of the interview accounts varied, something which the authors interpreted as a development generated by the reflections which the dialogue-oriented interviews had encouraged. Other interpretations are of course possible – perhaps that the interviewees adopted the norms which the researcher represented, or developed their ability to present coherent stories (which does not need to mean more 'true' or, still less, clearer or better-formulated-stories). A further possibility is that the interviewee did not want to repeat herself and may have modified accounts in order to make them interesting. It is, of course, also possible to emphasize the randomness of how accounts may develop. Recent experiences, the mood of the day, consumption of mass media reports with a bearing on the interview theme, how the interviewer starts, etc. – all this can lead to different outcomes in an interview situation. The point here is that the variations in accounts will often change over time and it is not a simple matter to interpret this.

In very ambitious efforts to establish contact over time and perhaps complement interviews with other methods (informal interaction, observations) it is not, however, impossible that a certain 'stabilization' of the meanings expressed by research subjects can appear (see Skeggs, 1997, for an account of such a research project). But it is often an open question as to what produces such stabilization and how can we understand it. It is not necessarily that the truth about the world out there or the meaning (truly and deeply) held by the respondent can account for this stability. Intensive interaction leading to the 'co-construction' of knowledge by researcher and interviewee can be an outcome of the idiosyncratic and highly local interplay of a debatable quality and value for moving outside this local setting.

Scheurich (1997) argues against the romantic, including advocates of the active interview ideal of the interviewer and interviewee working together in an open and productive manner to co-construct meaning. He claims that 'Interview interactions do not have some essential, teleological tendency toward an ideal of "joint construction of meaning"', irrespective of the intentions and skills of the researcher (p. 66). As will be substantiated below, interviews lend themselves to be managed only to a limited degree and all such efforts will create unforeseen complexities and side-effects. There are always sources of influence in an interview context that cannot be minimized or controlled. Turning up the room temperature from cold or lukewarm (neutral) to warm or even hot (very friendly) in an interview setting is not a straightforward way of accomplishing better interviews or producing more interesting and rich accounts.

The local setting and interaction always matter – irrespective of whether we think about 'cold' or 'lukewarm' interview situations (neo-positivist, structured, neutral). The major possible advantage of romantic research is instead that this kind of active approach may produce more varied and, therefore, more possible idea-stimulating talk. There are no safe procedures for sorting out low-quality from trustworthy and perceptive interview accounts in terms of their descriptive value. It is very difficult to avoid the 'problems' associated with the eight conceptualizations of interviews suggested in Chapter 5, indicating other logics and forces behind the production of interview accounts than interviewees' feelings and experience (Silverman, 2006).

The difficulties in finding a route to good results are indicated by the variety of advice for and criteria of good interview sessions also *within* the romantics' camp. All sorts of opinions exist about the appropriateness of an interviewer's direct involvement and degree of activity in the interview process. Ideas such as 'active interviewing' are not shared by other advocates of (un-structured) interviews. Many researchers suggest different interview styles. Miller and Glassner (1997), for example, propose neutrality as a suitable response to what interviewees are saying. They see a close interaction and trustbuilding with subjects as important but believe that one should hold back one's own opinions of interview accounts in the interaction. Kvale (1996) states that a criterion of a good interview is short questions followed by long answers, which presumably implies an interviewer who is withdrawn rather than active trying to put the interviewee in the centre. An interesting feature of the advice-giving literature on interviews is thus that it recommends different, even opposite moves. I think this supports a non-technical view on this subject matter – the 'solution' to interview problems is not found in a single best way or in a 'recipe' for how it should be done.

Localism

A still relatively small but growing option on interviewing breaks with the assumptions and purpose of neo-positivists and romantics. I refer to this as a *localist* position on interviewing. This approach emphasizes that interview statements must be seen in their local, situation-specific context. An interview is an empirical situation that can be studied as such and should not be treated as a tool for the collection of data on something existing outside this empirical situation. Localists do not ascribe to the interview an ontological status different from other events and situations. People talk with their neighbours, they serve customers at work, they go to the gym and they try to bring up their children. They also participate in interviews. Behaviour in interview situations can be studied in similar ways as these other phenomena:

> If the interview is a social encounter, then, logically, it must be analysed the same way as any other social encounter. The products of an interview are the outcome of a socially situated activity where the responses are passed through the role-playing and impression management of both the interviewer and the respondent. (Dingwall, 1997: 56)

An interview is often defined as a talk with a specific purpose, but even though the interviewer believes that the talk is formed by this purpose it is an open question whether the social situation is really subordinated to his/her intention.

Occasionally the interview has been studied as a social encounter, e.g. Schneider (2000) studied managers interviewing subordinates and, through their interviewing, producing a particular version of social reality. It is rare, however, that the research interview is addressed in this way any more than partially. Yes, many people may agree that the research interview is a social encounter, but think that it is clearly more than that – that it is tailored so that the interesting aspects move beyond the specifics of the local interaction appears to be a common view. The interviewer can thus shape the interview as his or her instruments, it is assumed.

In interviews, localists would argue, people are not reporting external events but producing situated accounts, drawing upon cultural resources in order to produce morally adequate accounts. Against the neo-positivist, and to a considerable extent also the romantic views on the interview as a technique, localists see it as situated accomplishment (Silverman, 1993: 104). As expressed by Potter (1997: 147) the 'social structure becomes part of interaction as it is worked up, invoked and reworked'. Sources of inspiration for localism include ethnomethodology, conversation and discourse analysis. Localism to some extent also shares certain features with poststructuralism/postmodernism, rejecting a mirror view on language and a humanistic view on the subject (Alvesson & Deetz, 2000; Rosenau, 1992). Both orientations view 'reality' as locally invented and reject the idea that language can communicate some essential meaning. Sometimes postmodernism in interview research is presented in a rather peculiar way, where the authentic voices of subjects are encouraged and allowed to come through, thus sounding more like hyper-romanticism than localism (and postmodernism with its scepticism of the view of the individual subject as a source of meaning and voice) (e.g. Fontana & Frey, 2005). Forms of localism like conversation and discourse analysis are, however, research programmes with a strong and specialised empirical focus and a rigorous methodology (Baker, 1997, 2003; Potter & Wetherell, 1987; Silverman, 1993, 2006). They differ then in vital respects from postmodernism, which typically favours more philosophical and often more playful ideas. Kilduff and Mehra (1997) identify five 'postmodern problematics': problematizing normal science, truth, representation, conventional styles of writing and generalizability. Silverman (1993), a leading representative of localism, takes a different position on virtually all those problematics, emphasizing the accumulation of knowledge, objectivity, the possibility of and very precise demands for representation, a clear writing style and the possibility of generalization. Here we find a sharp contrast between common postmodernist and localist research ideals. Localism can thus to some extent be connected to postmodernism but differences as well as similarities need to be considered.

The major problem with localism is of course that it involves a quite narrow research agenda. It trades relevance for rigour. It encourages a myopic interest in details around what is happening in the interview situation, which is studied as such, and it discourages treating what is being communicated as potentially important information for developing knowledge about broader phenomena, instead seeing it as no more than talk in interviews informed by cultural norms. The label of 'emotionalism' as used by Silverman (2006) indicates that the target of this scepticism is researchers' interest in feelings and authentic experiences. And the claim by some qualitative researchers that we may not gain objective reality, but rather the subjective views and meanings of people in interviews, is worthy of critique. It is not at all certain that interview statements reflect these often difficult to articulate views and meanings. It is sometimes easier to report on social events one has witnessed or one's behaviour than to describe feelings, cognitions and personal experiences. Interview talk may not reflect these often difficult to articulate aspects. Feelings, fantasies and experiences are not easy to express in words. So thus far I agree with Silverman. But irrespective of the problems of sometimes accessing people's subjective opinions or meanings, it is important to appreciate that interviews are not only used for studying highly personal issues. They are also used in order to get information about what is happening 'out there' – interviewees will report on social problems, decision making, city life, public sector reforms, organizational functioning, rescue operations and so on, areas where the interviewee is supposed to say something about things not necessarily close to their inner life or emotions. Reports about practices in a neighbourhood, in schools, workplaces, etc. may still be sensitive and include a strong personal element, and they may be difficult to talk accurately and neutrally about in interviews, but is not like reporting about one's self or other personally sensitive issues in relation to feelings for one's children or responses to sexual harassment. The critique of emotionalism (and to some extent romanticism more broadly) is not always directly relevant for addressing less personally sensitive issues.

Scepticism by localists can sometimes lead them to overshoot the target and reduce all interview talk to being contingent upon the local situation and bearing imprints of the inability of language to 'transport' meaning. A major purpose of this book is to develop interpretive strategies for increasing rigour but to retain relevance in interview-based research. Arguably, localist ideas need to be brought much more strongly into interview-based research, but we should not capitulate to the difficulties inherent in going beyond the interview situation in interpretations and the delivery of results.

Mixed positions

Within interview studies there have been efforts to consider both localist and romantic aspects. There is a partial appropriation of localist ideas in the interview literature oriented towards going beyond studying the setting. Gubrium and Holstein (1997: 114), for example, suggested that 'understanding *how* the meaning-making process unfolds in the interview is as critical as apprehending *what* is substantively asked and conveyed'. The interest in local circumstances and processes ('how') does not prevent these authors from believing in an ability within interview answers 'to convey situated experiential realities in terms that are locally comprehensible' (p. 117) and in interview subjects holding facts and details of experience, although in an interview a person 'constructively adds to, takes away from and transforms the facts and details' (p. 117). The interview then appears, on the whole, to be a valid source of knowledge-production, although the social process and local conditions need to be appreciated and actively managed by the interviewer in order to accomplish valid results. This makes sense but there are still problems, including an overestimation of the possibilities of sorting out the 'what' (substance, content, possibilities of accessing something 'outside' the interview) and the 'how' (talk contingent upon the situation and the use of conversation skills).

More generally within contemporary interview research there is sometimes an ambivalence and tension between a (mainly) romanticist conviction and a (partial) localist consideration. There can sometimes be a tendency to jump back and forth between quite varied positions. Fontana and Frey (2005: 719) are typical here when admitting that they 'share a concern with appreciating the new horizons of postmodernism while simultanously remaining conservatively committed to the empirical description of everyday life'. Perhaps we should not be too keen on being rigorous and coherent here and allow space for double positioning or at least ambivalence.

However, this position-jumping can often prove problematic, particularly if it is done without researchers being clear about it or explicit in communicating the shift between positions, i.e. between seeing interview accounts sometimes as reports with descriptive value, sometimes as 'only' local talk. It is tempting to be heavily influenced by postmodernists and localists on the one hand, avoiding any claim to capture the truth (outside the text/talk studied), but then still, on the other hand, reporting the truth (about things 'out there') in a straightforward way. An example here is Scheurich (1997: 67) who has argued against conventional views on interviews, emphasizing that the 'reality' of these is 'ambiguous, relative, and unknowable'. This has not prevented him from claiming that interviewees are active resistors of dominance by the interviewer and from stating that 'I have found this to be true in my own interviewing as a researcher'. He has also claimed that:

I find that interviewees carve out space of their own, that they can often control some or part of the interview, that they may push against or resist my goals, my intentions, my questions, my meanings. (1997: 71)

There is not much sign of the 'ambiguous, relative, and unknowable' in these 'Findings', which are presented as robust facts. Interpretations like 'carve out', 'control', 'push against' or 'resists' are seldom self-evident. On the other hand, Scheurich does limit his observations to the interview situation, perhaps going outside the domain of what is sayable according to postmodernism while keeping to the spirit of localism.

Advocates of narrative approaches will often also move between rather different positions in an ambiguous and even contradictory way. Riessman (2003), in an overview of interviews as personal narratives, claims for example that 'narrative analysis takes as its object of investigation the story itself' (p. 332), which would indicate a rather specific and narrow domain and not the moving outside of it.[4] But then what is being represented in the narratives 'tells us a great deal about social and historical processes', including contemporary beliefs (p. 353) and also 'individual and collective meanings, as well as the processes by which social life and human relationships are made and changed' (Laslett, cited in Riessman, 2003: 353). I am not necessarily doubting the possibility that narratives may be broadly informative, but there is a huge difference and a strong tension between focusing on an interview as a story to be studied as such and as telling us 'a great deal' about contemporary culture and the forming of social life and human relationships. This is common with varied and vague positioning regarding what is actually a narrative or story and whether – and if so how – it is possible to study it as such and/or then also to draw bold interpretations of 'extra-narrative' phenomena such as social conditions, culture, beliefs or even selves.

An example of the situation-specific interview research

Before moving on, perhaps it is necessary to illustrate that a more radical questioning of common (neo-positivist and romantic) views on the interviews is called for. Jorgenson (1991) provided a good example of the need to go beyond conventional approaches to interviews. Her research project was to understand how family members saw themselves as families and to get a sense of people's relational selves as members of a 'family'. Rather than leave it up to the researcher (family therapist, social worker, etc.) to define what a family was, it was seen as important to pay attention to how individuals in 'families' could understand themselves. This is a typical project for interview research, paying attention not to what experts decide to be the 'objective properties', but to the meanings and views of the subjects to be understood. This would be in line with unstructured and more or less romantic approaches. Jorgenson learned, perhaps hardly surprisingly, that individuals – and also those who see themselves as members of the same 'family' – will vary in terms of how they draw the boundaries between 'family' and 'non-family', and also in the criteria they will use in order to account for their distinctions.

One could end the story there, but Jorgenson noted and reflected upon some basic complexities in the research, making it difficult to simply claim that people have some ideas about 'family' and that the research showed these:

> The conceptualization of 'family' is, here, bound up in the process by which interviewer and respondent negotiate a sense of mutual understanding out of initially ambiguous questions and terms; and how they accomplish this cooperative construction, I would argue, depends on how they come to interpret each other as social actors. (1991: 215)

The respondents in turn partly produced accounts based on their shifting perceptions and understandings of the interviewer. Inconsistencies and apparent contradictions within specific interview accounts could then be understood not as 'errors', but as indications of the interpretative repertoires respondents would use when making sense of the person they were talking to. As an interviewer does not remain a constant during the interview – with the questions asked and the lines followed up, personal viewpoints expressed, etc. all affecting the construction of the person a respondent is talking to – variation can come through.

From a localist position this could be seen as an illustration of the futility of establishing fixed meanings, ideas or understandings that emerge from a stable relational self as a family member. 'Family' must be decentred and how it is constructed in various local, situation-specific settings needs to be considered. 'Family' becomes less a reflection of the unit 'out there' or fixed meanings (informed by authentic experiences) about 'it', than a matter of who is talking to who, in changing and varied ways, and how this is being done. There is a multitude of temporal, varying, sometimes inconsistent or even contradictory meanings in motion as 'family' is constructed and reconstructed in different situations. This variety and fluidity is not restricted to the interview situation, but can instead be traced to all kinds of situations and relations where 'family' becomes a topic (and presumably the same is so for childhood, consumption, travelling, views on environmental issues, attitudes to immigrants, etc.). We can, thus, perhaps study how talk about 'family' emerges and varies in an interview context, but using that interview as a clear pipeline to family as such or even to stable meanings held about situations appears more tricky. It is difficult to know if family talk with other people would be similar to or different from the talk produced in the context of an interview with a specific 'family researcher' (who, in the case here referred to, is also in communication studies, young, female, pregnant, white ...). Perhaps a different family researcher (older, in economics, gay, with an Arabic ethnicity ...) would trigger other conversations. And perhaps these interviews would look different depending on how and how much that age, economics, homosexuality, Arabic origin ... would be made explicit and emphasized in the interview (by the researcher and/or the interviewee).

Another illustration of the problems found when using interviews to access stable meanings or truths 'out there' can be found in Kvale (1996). This example is different in the sense that it non-voluntarily illustrates difficulties with interviews, i.e. the author is not indicating an awareness of problems. The situation I am discussing here was an interview about grades. The context was a seminar on method at a US university and the lecturer (Kvale himself) demonstrated an interview with a person in class who had volunteered for the task. The lecturer/ interviewer asked the student, in her thirties, 'Are you able to remember the first time you ever had any grades?' The student replies that she remembers one time 'Getting a red star on the top of my paper with 100; and that stands out in my memory as exciting and interesting'. The interview continues:

Interviewer: 'Yes, it is only the red star that stands out, or what happened around it?'

Student: (Laughter) 'I remember the color very very well. It was shining. I remember getting rewarded all the way around. I remember being honored by my classmates and the teacher and my parents – them making a fuss. And some of the other kids not responding so well who didn't do so well. It was mixed emotions, but generally I remember the celebration aspect.'

Interviewer:	'You said mixed emotions. Are you able to describe them?'
Student:	'Well, at that time I was a teacher's pet and some people would say, "aha, maybe she didn't earn it, maybe it is just because the teacher likes her so well". And some kind of stratification occurring because I was not only the teacher's pet but I was getting better grades and it created some kind of dissonance within my classmates' experience of me socially.
Interviewer:	'Could you describe that dissonance?'
Student:	'Well, I think there's always some kind of demarcation between students who do well and students who don't do as well, and that's determined, especially in the primary grades, by the number that you get on top of your paper'. (Kvale 1996: 136–137).

The interview continues but we don't need to follow it any longer here as it mainly repeats and varies the theme of interpersonal tensions. This interview is presented in the book as an example of how an interview should be conducted and it gives a competent and convincing impression. As a reader one is probably inclined to accept the data indicating that in this case the grades led to interpersonal tensions and some problems for the interviewee. I would not argue that this is not trustworthy, but there is still a strong element of randomness in how the interview goes. The interviewer draws attention to and asks the interviewee to describe 'mixed emotions'. This seems to trigger an inclination to emphasize the negative side of getting a red star. The rest of the interview then follows this line of description, where 'demarcation' and 'space between me and the peer group' are mentioned. The negative experience comes out quite clearly. However, this may be an affect of the attention paid to 'mixed emotions' – a signifier often pointing to the negative aspects. When the interviewer singles out these words and asks the interviewee to elaborate on this, it may be read as encouraging the interviewee to focus on the downside of things. This then dominates the rest of the interview and the impression is that the grade affected the person mostly in a negative way.

However, in the interview there are indications of this not necessarily being the most significant emotion. As seen above, the interviewee starts by saying the event 'stands out in my memory as exciting and interesting'. She also says that 'I remember being honored by my classmates ...' and that she responded like this: 'It was mixed emotions, but generally I remember the celebration aspect'. If the interviewer had picked out any of the other ingredients in the statements than 'mixed emotions' (e.g. asking if she could develop what was meant by generally remembering the celebration aspect or that getting the red star stands out in the memory as exciting and interesting) then the interviewee may had developed these quite differently and other impressions of dominating emotions and meanings would have been conveyed. This is not to say that the interview did not reveal important findings, but there is a possibility that the interviewee, given other interventions by the researcher, would have told a quite different story. Also, with 'being honored by classmates' the mixed emotions regarding negative responses are not entirely coherent, so the theme of classmate responses could have moved in different directions if focused upon in a slightly different way during the interview. That 20–25 years has passed since the event may also make the interviewee sensitive to clues about how to remember the situations.

One could add that the researcher himself was a strong believer in the negative effects of grades and that this may have informed both the question asked and to some extent also the interview response. A researcher with a strong belief in the positive functions of grade may have paid more attention to the positive emotions reported. There is no way to determine what is the best or what is true here. It is difficult to ask the interviewee to describe in more detail any emotion or meaning expressed – this easily leads to very long and complicated interviews and the first question asked may have had a steering effect anyway. So regardless of whichever of the interview claims about 'mixed emotions' or 'generally I remember the celebration aspect' had been first chosen for exploration, this probably would have affected the response to the other.

My point here is that interviews are complex and thus it is not easy to extract some true meaning or objective fact from the talk produced. Even an expert on interviews like Kvale (1996) may not be entirely aware of exactly what is happening and may, more or less voluntarily, be involved in producing interview effects as subtle outcomes of expectations or specific interventions. Whether the interview reveals the truth about some external reality or stable personal meaning/ experience or whether it reflects more the local dynamics and contingencies of the interview situation is then open to question.

The interviewer and interviewee as the source of 'problems'

We can expand the critique and scepticism of the localism of technical and instrumental views of interviews by pointing towards the complications associated with the interviewer, the interviewee, and the social situation.

Many researchers view the interviewer's handling of a situation as the key element in interviews. Charmaz (2003: 317), for example, assumes that 'an interviewer's questions and interviewing style shape the context, frame and content of the study'. She emphasizes how 'framing questions takes skill and practice' and warns against asking the wrong questions, stressing the need to ask questions that 'both explore the interviewer's topic and fit the participant's experience' (p. 315). Here the competent interviewer who is designing and conducting the interview is the central ingredient for having good control over the situation and producing worthwhile data.

Other researchers are less confident about the interviewer being the subject in full control and also view the other participant (the interviewee) as having a crucial and not so straightforward role. As Scheurich (1997: 62) points out 'the researcher has multiple intentions and desires, some of which are consciously known and some of which are not. The same is true of the interviewee'. Many researchers probably think this is an exaggeration of the problems and an underestimation of the competently carried-through interview and might therefore tend to construct the researcher-interviewer (i.e. themselves) as well as the interviewee in more positive terms, assuming that they are both basically engaged in the knowledge-pursuing project and are capable of mobilizing a reasonable degree of rationality and control. Some researchers would agree with the view of the subjects' involvement in the interview as being far from rational but would also assume the intellectual and theoretical capacity of a researcher to master the situation:

> We intend to construe both researcher and researched as anxious, defended subjects, whose mental boundaries are porous where unconscious material is concerned. This means that both will be subject to projections and introjections of ideas and feelings coming from the other person. (Hollway & Jefferson, 2000: 45)

This may sound alarming, but Hollway and Jefferson believe that psychoanalysis and narrative analysis make it possible to understand the research relationship and that guided by this support paying attention to the researcher's own feelings becomes a valuable aid in interpreting the subject matter. While one may applaud such recognition of the role of feelings as well as of the complexity of the research situation, one may be doubtful about the full possibilities of interpreting the situation as well as the use of psychoanalytic and narrative theory as a means of clarification and raising the researcher up to a higher standard. Once again the problems produced by going radically outside the local situation and context-specific storytelling are not easy to handle.

Interviewee motives

Generally speaking, authors on the research interview see the interviewee's response as mainly an outcome of the researcher's framing of the situation, asking and following up of questions, establishing confidence, etc. However, the interviewee may be far less compliant or able to mobilize for truth-seeking projects. The romantic view on interviewing is grounded in an image of a potentially honest, unselfish subject, eager or at least willing to share his or her experiences and knowledge for the benefit of the interviewer and the research project. The interviewee then supposedly acts in the interests of science. The view of the interviewee as an informant illustrates this assumption. However, interviewees may have other interests than assisting science by simply providing information. They may be *politically aware and politically motivated actors*. Many people will have a political interest in how socially significant issues are represented. This does not necessarily mean that they will cheat or lie. Honesty and political awareness do not necessarily conflict. In addition, some respondents not using the interview mainly for their own political purposes may very well tell the (partial) truth as they know it but in favourable ways for them and may not disclose truths disfavourable either to them or their group. Plus the interviewees may have problems expressing reliable knowledge (or data that can be refined to knowledge) because of the difficulties in translating their version of the world into the interview context.

Interviewees may not know that much or they may have problems in communicating what they do know in 60 minutes to, in most cases, a complete stranger. In some scenarios interviewees will feel an expectation to know as well as to tell – 'what are your attitudes, motives, thoughts about … and … ?' – and may then try to invent something in order to satisfy the requirements of the interviewer and fill the role called for by the interview situation.

The tricky relationship between 'knowing' and 'telling'

The interviewee may be problematic because s/he may actually be 'knowing' but may be incapable of 'telling'. People may also of course – for good or less good reasons – be capable but unwilling to tell, but my point here is about the difficulties of expressing knowledge in words. A lot of our knowledge is tacit and hard to articulate. People can be more clever than their ability to use words would indicate. They may know something but cannot express it very well, at least not in a brief interview talk with a stranger. We may be altogether incapable of communicating something on a difficult topic or this may come out as vague, clumsy and confused when we try to do so.

People may also be willing to tell or capable of telling something convincing, but *not* actually knowing. Interviewees may use words correctly and credibly, but this may not reflect anything outside competent language use. The interviewee asked about her experiences of her first grade referred to above. She talks in a way that appears trustworthy, but is her memory of her response 20–25 years ago reliable? A teacher may speak convincingly about her progressive pedagogy, but the deeper knowledge or practices based thereupon may be lacking.[5] When conducting interviews with managers many can produce a suitable story for themselves as 'leaders' doing 'leadership', but this often seems to say more about them having participated in management education and read about the topic in the mass media than them actually having put this in action and practised living up to this talk (Alvesson & Sveningsson, 2003). The managers seemed to come across as much more advanced in interview talk than in their practices. Talk indicated leadership as working with values, visions and strategies, while practices seemed to be more about sitting in meetings and dealing with administrative and operative problems. In this case the discrepancy was very strong and we as researchers were also quite open to the possibility of ambiguity and incoherence so this came out also in the interpretations of the interviews, but often interviewees can be capable of appearing coherent and so incoherencies are sometimes easily missed by researchers eager to find patterns. Sometimes researchers want to marginalize or go beyond a 'surface variation or inconsistency' and find an underlying coherence. Most leadership research emphasizes leadership styles, values and types, or something else which is coherent and integrated.

In other words, people may be smarter at using words than showing who they really are or how they really act. This may be an effect of an interview society: here we know how to talk and give an impression of knowing through following the right conventions, but we may not actually 'know' the things we talk about or be capable of delivering in practice what we are capable of producing credible conversations about. Of course often the practice is talk, but there is a difference between talking about one's practices in interviews (or speeches) and then talking-in-practice, partly as the latter involves more than 'just the talk' as it relates to specific situations and material actions as well. Therefore people may be more competent in interview talk than in everyday-action contexts, where talk is important but other issues are also involved.

Sometimes in research indications of *not* knowing will emerge. And even if a statement is produced – perhaps as a response to the expectation to know and be able to come up with a clear answer – one may decide to take uncertainties around such statements seriously. Yet this is often not the case. Researchers will often have an interest in producing positive results and may then downplay any signs of uncertainty, including when interviewees are possibly not in the know. In a study of young Somalis in Norway briefly mentioned above, the author refers to an interviewee who 'defines herself as more Somali than Norwegian'. The person says: 'I feel both, but most Somali, I think' (Fangen, 2007: 405). The added 'I think' statement may signal that the interviewee does not really know – and often we may not know how we feel in relation to social categories. Such feelings may vary between different situations and may be more of a process than stable attributes. The statement is nevertheless interpreted as knowing and as producing a valid answer allowing for the clear-cut statement by the researcher that 'she defines herself as more Somali than Norwegian' (p. 405). Of course, even if the person had not added 'I think' there is no reason to take the statement at face value as an expression of knowledge. In the study, the person was presumably addressed (or experienced herself) as a young Somali in Norway (the topic of the study) interviewed by a native Norwegian, possibly underscoring a particular view of her self-definition but not necessarily the one dominating in other situations.

We thus have the problem of a possible incongruence between what our interviewees may know and what they may be able (or willing) to express. Class matters here of course. Upper-class people, with a higher education and jobs in which language use and symbolism are central, are often more skilled with words than people with less education and manual jobs. The latter will sometimes perform badly in interviews. For the former, words may often be smarter than people (and their practices), for the latter people (and their practices) may be smarter than their use of words in interviews may indicate.

The interviewee is thus a difficult part of interview work. There are no easy tricks to resolving this. Interventions from the interviewer to increase motivation or the ability to tell or explore whether the interviewee 'really' knows can be productive but can also complicate issues: the interviewee may follow the interviewer's cues or become defensive and act 'safely' if the interviewer explores whether the interview talk is really founded on 'facts' (true experiences, actual trustworthy observations or whatever is at stake). If the interviewer asks for 'proofs' – specific examples – on the issues the interviewee is claiming at a more general level, the respondent may be able to find something broadly in line with this and then construct this in a way that seems to illustrate an overall value or competence. We can all come up with credible examples of our fine qualities or values in terms of working, being anti-racist, aware of sex roles, good parenting, having integrity, etc. The interviewer may do the 'right' things (following the template of an interview technique book), but this may not be a guarantee for finding out if the person who seems to know really does know or not.

The interview situation as a 'problem'

Apart from those 'problems' associated with the interviewer and the interviewee we also need to consider the difficulties associated with the *situation* as such, i.e. not only uncertainties about researcher intervention tactics or interviewees being unmotivated or incapable of telling (or telling without really knowing), but also with the setting and interactions. The interview situation is, under the surface, quite complicated. Two strangers are supposed to get an understandable and valid summary of some key aspects of a targeted set of practices and/ or experiences of these (I will come back to the complexities at length later in the book). There is considerable focus in the method literature on how to 'manage' the interview situation, i.e. to make it as rational and productive as possible through effective interviewer behaviour or showing how to create good and close contact, making people open up and be authentic. Sometimes these tactical considerations are broadened to consider the interview as a complex social setting that the interviewer may be unable to control. This would imply that the researcher should not just focus on questions and answers but should also keep an eye on the dynamics of the interaction of which s/he is a part. Small wonder that so many interviewers will feel exhausted after a few hours of interview work.

Sometimes involving more than one researcher in an interview can been seen as a potential solution. Eisenhardt (1989), for example, recommends that there are two interviewers present – one asking questions and the other making observations of what is happening – in order to reduce interviewer subjectivity and bias. The advantages are obvious in the sense that the observing researcher can have another overview and be distanced from what is happening and not be caught up in the immediate interaction. The person mainly observing can intervene at times and increase the 'rationality' of the situation. But there are also problems involved. One obvious disadvantage is the extra cost (time). More relevant to consider in the context of this book is perhaps that being observed by a fairly passive person increases the social complexity of the situation for the interviewee. The situation with one active interviewer and one passive observer then may be experienced as similar to a police interrogation which would nicely illustrate Foucault's view of the power/knowledge connection in social inquiry – the interview being a site for surveillance and control through making people's thoughts, experiences, emotions and beliefs public and therefore an object for potential control by companies, the state or whoever may have the resources to exploit the control potential that follows on from social inquiry. This point of course goes far beyond Eisenhardt's suggestion but her specific argument fits nicely into, and reminds us about, a wider set of issues. One may speculate whether a passive observer being present during an interview may make the interviewee (even more) inclined to give safe and correct answers, as being observed (monitored) by a third person may add to the anxiety of the situation. Eisenhardt disregards the impact of the social setting on the interviewee, with the consequence that the responses remain partly outside of a researcher's control.

So, as with the adding on of a second interviewer (observer), technical operations may have unintended effects. This is presumably the case with all interventions. Ways to solve problems or reduce uncertainties may lead to unexpected complexities and responses that researchers cannot control.

In addition to looking at the specific actors involved and focusing on the local social situation it is important to broaden the perspective and examine the overall context to frame what is directly observable. Such a broader perspective takes into account the ordering principles that may be in operation and that in various ways guide or control the interview interaction and the 'data' produced. The social situation is not just a meeting between two or several people, but also takes place in a societal, cultural and political context. Various macro forces – including the assumptions and norms of our 'interview society' and the idea that one should be genuinely personal and reveal one's self while not hiding behind roles or conventions (Sennett, 1977) – operate behind the interview as a micro situation. These may easily be missed if one is only concentrating on the micro situation and the subjects and local interactions visible within it. How cultural and discursive themes may operate behind subjects' backs is difficult to investigate, possibly calling for a broader consideration than only putting one's magnifiers on the actual talk produced in the setting at hand. Of course this is a difficult topic and sceptics with a strong empiricist leaning may reject what is not directly visible in the data as pure speculation and instead focus on 'data' in the form of interview material and then, perhaps, 'minimize the violence' (Pratt, 2009: 499). But when all our energy is put into producing, codifying, analysing and reporting such material, it is easy to miss or marginalize a careful appreciation of the uncertainty of the material for the (false) comfort of a naïve empiricism.

The state of the art

While recognizing the difficulties inherent in neatly ordering a field and identifying its clear trends, I will nevertheless suggest some over-all aspects of the current situation in interview-based research. Developments in interview methods have to some extent moved from neo-positivist conceptions to an increased awareness of the complexity of the interview situation, including a need to gain the full cooperation of interviewees. And yet a lot of the literature on interviewing continues to deal at length with how this practice may be utilized as effectively as possible and how to get the interview subject to talk a lot (but perhaps not too much, as the interviewer would normally like to cover a number of sub-themes in limited time) as well as openly, trustingly, honestly, clearly and freely about what the researcher is interested in. Most writers on interviews, despite signalling their awareness of complications, seem to assume that skills may be developed and an approach taken in which errors are minimized (or at least the problems and contingen-cies are handled) and qualified empirical material is produced (see for example Charmaz, 2003; Easterby-Smith et al., 1991; Fontana & Frey, 1994, 2005; Kvale, 1996). Tapping interviewees for knowledge continues to be the major purpose and outcome of interview research. This is more clearly pronounced in the research literature using interviews in empirical studies than in the sometimes more 'progressive' or sophisticated texts on methodology addressing the interview.

Published research reporting on interview-based studies frequently lacks references to reflexive or philosophical literature and often expresses neo-positivist positions. In general, interview accounts are presented as data pointing toward a particular reality and very little space is typically used to discuss the weaknesses and problems of linking accounts with some interior or exterior reality. In the study of young Somalis in Norway briefly mentioned above, for example, all interview accounts are presented as directly reflecting how the interviewees related to and acted in relation to the issues addressed, i.e. ethnicity and culture (Fangen, 2007). It is claimed one of those interviewed, Hassan, 'has changed to a more individualized practice of religion. Religion keeps him from gossiping about people and from getting angry. Thus, religion is a guiding principle for actions and a mediative way to handle problems and conflicts' (p. 407). It is of course possible that this is 'objectively' the case or that Hassan himself believes this, but it is not easy to say this based on the interview alone. Perhaps the interview talk reflects a norm of emphasizing individuality or is constructed to provide a positive view of practitioners of Islam in light of contemporary suspicion in the Western world. Perhaps Hassan seriously believes all he said, at least in the interview situation, but people following him at close range may have perceived his development differently. It is hard to know here, but the paper does not address this issue.

It is not uncommon to express an awareness of the problem of addressing interview statements as true and of claims to avoid treating the material as if this were the case, but not really sticking to this position and sometimes treating statements as indications of how 'it is'. In a paper on female entrepreneurs (perhaps better described as small business-owners) of Turkish and Moroccan origin in the Netherlands, the authors glide between quite different knowledge claims. They 'stress that these narratives reflect neither the female entrepreneurs of Turkish and Moroccan origins' multiple identities nor their lived realities, but are linguistic constructions made in close interaction with the researcher' (Essers & Benschop, 2007: 56). They also, however, write

35

that the central question is that of how these female entrepreneurs 'construct their professional identities from two cultural contexts in dialogue with relevant others' and study 'the lived practices' and 'how the social categories of entrepreneurship, gender and ethnicity are negotiated in the construction of professional identities and how these identities are embedded in power relations' (p. 50). The presented interview statements are then mainly addressed as if they reflected the life situations of those interviewed and how they experience these situations and see themselves. This is of course fully possible – and the paper in many ways gives a good impression – but what is said in the interviews may also reflect conventions for interview talk or considerations of the impression the interviewees want to accomplish. The paper, like many other contemporary writings, moves ambiguously between different purposes and knowledge claims, contingent upon quite different meanings attributed to the interview material. The meanings span from 'linguistic constructions made in close interaction with the researcher' to clear and straightforward indicators on how the identities of those being studied are actually constructed in practice. The distance between the former and the latter can be considerable, partly fuelled by a possible wish to present oneself in a specific way in relation to the politically contested macro cultural and political situation influencing the interview context (mentioned by the authors). The anticipation of reactions and how talk feeds into more or less favourable views of the group studied are particularly central in socially sensitive and contested areas like immigration and ethnicity, although it is of course very difficult to assess the possible relevance of such considerations in Essers and Benschop's study (and similar ones such as the paper on Somalis in Norway addressed above). In the case of Essers and Benschop there is an acknowledgement that the interviews may not reflect some external reality, mixed up with what seems to be an ambition to deliver clear results, thus leading to ambivalence and inconsistency. This is not uncommon.

Apart from recognizing the overall politics in society influencing interviewees, some researchers consider political aspects in a much more local setting. Some interview-based studies as well as parts of the methodological literature for example refer to the political dimensions of qualitative research in specific institutional settings such as organizations (e.g. Easterby-Smith et al., 1991; Parker, 2000). In case studies of workplaces and institutions, issues around dependencies and direct sanctions plus problems surrounding anonymity add to the complexity of the situation. Those interviewed belong to the same social setting and interview statements can be read by the people talked about or responsible for conditions addressed in interviews. Sometimes they can actually be identified by other insiders, even despite researchers' best efforts to guarantee anonymity. Even if the interviewer is eager to reassure interviewees that there should not be anything 'objectively' to worry about, interviewees may be cautious. There is always some uncertainty involved. Awareness of the ethics and politics of research has probably been developed over the years, but a greater appreciation of the subtleties of the political aspects and not just the research as a whole as well as what takes place in the interview situation is sometimes lacking in studies as well as method literature.

Another line of development is an increasing interest in reflexivity in the sense of exploring the relationship between researchers and the knowledge production. Reflexivity is of course important here (e.g. Fine et al., 2000; Reinharz, 1997; Steier, 1991). Reflexivity in an interview context has included more of a focus on the researcher's part and less on how to understand the interview situation and the interviewee as a 'knowing subject' which is so central in interview-based knowledge production. As will be developed later (especially in Chapter 6), I am talking about reflexivity in another sense – as less focused on the researcher as a person. I think it is more important to consider the research perspective, language and line of interpretation, which often have less to do with the individual researcher's subjectivity than the ways of reasoning and ordering the world as favoured by a specific research camp (paradigm, theoretical school). Reflexivity then addresses discourse, theory and interpretation more than the specific researcher involved, even though one can't fully separate the person and theoretical practice. The interview literature seldom incorporates any ambitious theoretical ideas on these subject matters and tends to treat them as a bias to be overcome with techniques or as something to be aware of in analysis. The possibility that political or social issues make the phenomena studied contested terrain and the interviews strongly affected by this is often marginalized or trivialized. Or simply denied.

Academic journal publication conventions tend to domesticate scholarly writing so that research texts will sometimes contradict the espoused anti-positivist theoretical orientation of many qualitative researchers (Briggs, 2003: 500). For example, some studies drawing on Foucauldian and other poststructuralist ideas ironically rest on 'depersonalized, third-person and apparently objective and authoritative representations' (Wray-Bliss, 2002: 20) – representations that go against a Foucauldian understanding of how 'knowledge' is always related to power and a will to order and control the world. Increasingly, however, authors will include remarks signalling caution, e.g. they will use such expressions as interviewees 'reported such feelings' (Martin et al., 1998) or 'gave me this account' (Barker, 1993: 408), or they will express some modesty in the claims of a study, such as 'ours are but provisional interpretations ... ' (Covalski et al., 1998: 308). Still, such signalling only marginally softens an impression of the data and results on the whole being presented as robust and authoritative: the reader is no more than moderately encouraged to reflect upon the meanings of interviews and what the accounts are really about.

A journal format and readers general impatience probably drive many authors to some form of neo-positivism. In reports of empirical research, the reader wants (or is anticipated to want) a brief, concise and convincing method section. What was done in the research work, how the empirical material was analysed and how the researcher arrived at the research result and conclusion are questions that are supposed to be answered in a distinct and straightforward way. Transparency and a clear logic and procedure are called for. This probably often forces researchers to partly fake their method section, as little research is probably done in such a neat and linear way. If interviews varied heavily due to a local interaction – as advocated by romanticists – then it is even more difficult and space-consuming to report on what was done, how the 'data' were 'collected'. (Collected is perhaps not the best label here, as will be addressed in the next chapter, but there is sometimes an expectation to use it as part of a rational and linear research process.) It is also very difficult to provide a brief and convincing account for data processing and analysis. Highly diverse material cannot be easily codified, categorized, compared and aggregated. And the data reported are supposed to be clear and convincing, leaving limited space for raising doubts and reflections about whether interview data (or questionnaire responses) say anything about what goes on 'out there', outside of the interview conversation or questionnaire filling-in exercise. So the rules for writing about methods and reporting empirical material in research applications also tend to reinforce a view on interview material that is in line with neo-positivism or possibly a constrained version of rational interactionism.

Interview work and its results may therefore often be followed up by writings that give a polished, perhaps even a distorted view of the research and the role of interviews in it. But even if researchers adapt their writing to the standards for reporting rather than telling the true story, the standards imposed by most journals still mean that interview researchers may be pushed away from the warmer forms of romanticism (or loosely structured interviewing more generally). Journal standards may influence not only writing but also how research actually is done. There may of course be variations across disciplines, but generally I think that journal publication formats reinforce research approaches that are not too difficult to account for. Published work is a strong norm-setter for researchers and may in this sense override the methodological literature that warns against using interview material as a simple indicator on reality and a building bloc for theory.

Of course, all this does not imply that qualitative researchers generally are neo-positivist empiricists believing that interviews are undertaken in a rational, standardized manner or that the resulting data set produced speaks for itself. There is a general recognition that data are about constructions and must be interpreted. Still, interview accounts are seen as providing clues – perhaps indirect and uncertain, but still clues – to the 'interiors' of the interviewees or the 'exteriors' of social practices (meaning respectively facts). In order to be more open towards the option that interview statements reveal less about these phenomena and more about something else, e.g. behaviour in interview settings, I will suggest a variety of different theoretical conceptualizations of the research interview and its dynamics (see Chapter 4).

Conclusion: taking localism seriously – but not too seriously

I think it is important to consider carefully ideas coming from postmodernism, localism and other orientations that raise doubts about the interview as a means for producing knowledge, but to balance these also with considerations of social relevance and not necessarily giving priority to a methodological precision in social science. I would argue for a broader and somewhat looser orientation than the rather narrow, even myopic view favoured by localists while sharing their concerns about the need to improve our methodological consciousness and about being much more careful when working with empirical material than is often the case in the interview society. (Something similar can be said about a questionnaire-filling society as well, for that matter – many of the problems arising with a naïve view on data are of course even worse in quantitative studies, but this is not my concern here.) My basic position is one that holds with a philosophically up-dated interpretive social science that favours a careful interpretation in which ambiguity and the impossibility of finding an ultimate truth or a best interpretation are acknowledged. Research practices like decon-struction are often useful for exploring weakly grounded claims and for considering alternative ways of interpretation, but should be used with moderation (Alvesson, 2002; Alvesson & Sköldberg, 2009).

Often interview researchers will reject the idea of the interview being similar to other conversations by referring to their purpose and a researcher's use of a situation. But can a researcher maintain that much control over a setting? My answer is perhaps not: many more intellectual resources than are commonly used need to be mobilized and a careful interpretation carried out before researchers can make a good case for the specific purposes that interview material can actually be used for – beyond studying our use of conversational skills in interview contexts.

The localist approach to interviewing is basically a critical one: it challenges the assumptions, claims and purpose of those wanting to use interviews instrumentally (Silverman, 1993, 2006). Its proponents generally favour 'naturally occurring interaction', but interviews can also be used as objects of study for detailed discourse or conversation analysis. This may appear as narrow and myopic, if not downright odd and trivial, especially for those taking it for granted that interviews are tools for accessing data, but there are some interesting options here to which I shall return in the final parts of the book. Critiquing localism for its rather narrow focus and its underestimation of seeing interview-ees as potentially knowledgable subjects able to communicate impor-tant insights about their social reality is, I think, understandable. Localism comes close to denying the possibility of exploring meaning and the 'native's point of view'. But it is crucial for social science to use interviews for studying people's understandings of the meanings in their lived world, describing their experiences and self-understanding and clarifying and elaborating their own perspectives on their lived world (Kvale, 1996: 105). Despite many expressions of interviews being somewhat naïve, this is not a motivation for writing off inter-views as a site for communicating valuable research material.

The three ideal-typical positions on interviews addressed in this chapter (and I see interactive rationalism as an 'in-between-form', sometimes bordering on neo-positivism, sometimes on romanticism) do not do full justice to the variety of views of interviewing expressed in the method literature and social research, but do indicate the broader orientations that most qualitative researchers using interviews as their principle method would subscribe to. My ambition is to move beyond these. I am, to some extent, drawing upon localism in a critique of the two dominant positions on interviews, but will also take issue with localist ideas in trying to save some version of a 'tool' view on interviews and also on using the interview as a site for exploring broader issues than merely talk in an interview situation, without falling too deeply into the trap of viewing interview talk as a representation of the interiors of subjects or the exteriors of the social worlds they participate in.

I will argue that we need a set of reference points for thinking through the interview situation and its use in interpretation. This can sharpen our thinking on what can and cannot be extracted from interview talk in research. This means embracing some complexity when compared to the common views presented above. This will easily add pressure on the sagging shoulders of the interview researcher, who will also have other worries than levels of methodological sophistication, including the challenge of producing some interesting results. Using metaphors is helpful for structuring thinking and remembering key points and the next chapter discusses the advantages (and disadvantages) of doing so.

Notes

1   The literature reviewing qualitative research is also of limited relevance for this book, as this typically focuses on paradigms or broad schools and seldom says that much about research practices. It divides up the field in different ways (e.g. Alvesson & Sköldberg, 2009; Delanty, 2005; Denzin & Lincoln, 1994, 2005; Guba & Lincoln, 1994). In identifying major positions to interviewing, it makes sense to move somewhat closer to the level of research practice than what is signalled by the reference to broad paradigms. In many cases, the mentioned broader streams, e.g. critical theory, include little of distinct perspectives on interviews.

2   I will not refer more than marginally to this position later in this book as I think that the positions identified by Silverman, and implicitly

reproduced/confirmed by most of the interview methodologists arguing against neo-positivism, capture orientations that are useful to relate to in clarifying alternative standpoints. While many researchers are not extremely neo-positivistic or romantic most will tend to go in one or other of these directions.

3   There are also some theoretically more specialized notions of interviewing, drawing upon a narrative theory of the whole or gestalt of the story and psychoanalytical ideas of the defensive self that call for an interview technique and a way of interpretation in order to get to the subject beneath what is espoused (e.g. Hollway & Jefferson, 2000). This approach differs from romanticism in some ways, but shares with it a belief in accessing empirical material being highly informative about the interviewee and that interview table reflects the self of the interviewee.

4   This is in contrast to researchers that use the stories as vehicles to get into the lives of those studied, e.g. Hollway and Jefferson (2000: 32) who state that they focus on 'the people that tell us stories about their lives; the stories themselves are a means to understand our subjects better'.

5   One often sees a version of this in academic writings, where the researcher, particularly if it is a PhD student, feels committed to interpretive/ constructionist/critical methodology and expresses this in e.g. Chapter 2 of a thesis, but then does mainly conventional, neo-positivist work in the major part of the study, addressing phenomena in a thing-like, objectivist manner. This is sometimes undetected by the PhD student and the supervisor.

3

PRACTICAL ASPECTS ON INTERVIEW STUDIES

As should be clear by now I don't see the practical or theoretical sides of interview studies as the most important to address, at least not in terms of specific suggestions for how to do things. This does, of course, not mean that they are insignificant. To plan and carry out interviews in a good manner is a precondition for getting a material worth interpreting. It is certainly a challenge to produce a clever design and effectively execute an interview study – as is the case with other qualitative investigations. There are many important questions around the design and tactics of a study, the choice of interviewees, to secure access to these, to use interview time efficiently, to try to minimize unnecessary imperfections (type making interviewees excessively careful or asking leading questions or allow them talking about irrelevant things). There are also insecurities around choice of the possible use of technical equipment, how to deal with transcripts, how to sort the material so it becomes more manageable ('data management') and through this sorting get some help with direction with analysis, how to relate to those being studied when the interview (or research project) is to be finished, etc. I don't see these technical and practical aspects as the most important to address in a fairly advanced method book, compared to intellectually much more demanding issues such as how to understand the interview situation and the nature of the talk produced. The technical and practical can in most cases be dealt with through common sense and situational adaptation to the specific area of study and the specific investigation. Often the researcher has to try and see what works in practical situations.

This is not to say that it is without interest to also address some important aspects on the practice of designing and carrying out interviews. This will be done fairly briefly in this chapter. I do only moderately connect directly to the various perspectives on interviews addressed in the previous chapter, but have in mind a kind of average or typical view on the interview, somewhere in between neo-positivism and romanticism, e.g. as exemplified above as interactive rationalism and involving a 'medium' level of structure (or specification in terms of the questions asked). The chapter starts with a brief argumentation against a strong focus on technical knowledge on interviews, before moving over to addressing some central aspects of the interview process.

On the need of technical–practical perspectives on the interview – or beyond 'tape-recorder knowledge'

There is a wealth of technically and practically oriented books on how to do interviews. It is possible to read about how to approach interviewees and what is worth considering when producing the interview transcripts. A lot of all this is on a tape-recorder technique level and includes plenty of good advice, such as that one should be dressed properly in order to not alienate the interviewees. If you, for example, want to interview old people in the Conservative party about moral decay you would be wise not approaching them in patched jeans and with a large ring in the nose. Practical advice may be valuable but can be addressed through the use of one's own judgement and through learning from practical experience, perhaps in informal talks with colleagues. That something is important does not imply that you have to spend many pages in a book on the topic. Interviewing as a practical activity is a bit like dinner conversations, cycling and sex: important and not always easy, but perhaps not something that you primarily learn to master through reading books.

Some authors are eager to bring forward their personal experiences based on various projects. The personal is certainly central in all research, in particular of a qualitative nature. There are often considerable individual variations in specific studies making the exact way the study took place difficult to describe in ways particularly relevant for larger groups of readers, unless of course one writes for a highly specialized audience. If somebody, for example, writes about the work with an interpreter in interviewing individuals in a village in a, for the researcher, exotic country where people are unfamiliar with interviews as a practice and there is considerable confusion of what it is all about, this can be interesting to read about but the value for the large majority of all those doing interviews in 'interview society' may be limited. So may also be the case with questions regarding personal safety for the interviewer if the job is carried out in dangerous slum areas or with members of criminal gangs. And difficulties in balancing firmness, diplomacy and appropriate subordination in interviews with individuals from the highest elite, customed to control the agenda and being skilful in using situations to their own advantage and avoiding exposure to potential critique, include interesting method problems. But to consider these may be of limited usefulness for the large majority of all researchers that are not in the business of trying to get valuable information from people in this exclusive and difficult to handle group. (I tried to interview an ex-minister once, assuming that several years after retirement he would be quite open about things. He had also read one of my books and invited me to give a talk based on it, so I thought the precondition for a good and 'deep' interview about his experiences on certain issues was favourable. But he avoided or reformulated my questions and responded as an active politician in front of a TV camera – only providing 'bullet-proof' statements. All my efforts in opening up or bypassing the armour of the 'respondent' – or rather, in this case the non-respondent, were in vain. Interesting, perhaps, but I don't think we can learn that much from the example. All my 'tricks' failed too, but this does not say that they could not work in similar interview situations.) Specific experiences are important, but can be rather idiosyncratic and of marginal value for others if they don't exemplify a broader aspect. The advantage with the theoretical ideas brought forward in this book is that they, being more abstract and theoretical, have a broader relevance and can contribute to lift and qualify thinking and sharpen interview work independently of what one, more exactly, is interested in studying.

My view is that method books perhaps do not have to focus so much on the technical, practical or personal as is common but should put much more emphasis on how to understand and interpret the interview situation and what comes out of this. It is demanding to get a good intellectual and theoretical understanding of the interview method and I suggest that an advanced framework is the most important support for interview based research that moves clearly beyond a journalistic approach. It is thus theoretical qualification and critical thinking that the present book primarily offers. The practical relevance of this is strong, from how you think through what you want and are able to study, how you prepare and act in the interview to how you interpret and re-interpret the material. In particular Chapters 6 and 7 address this. But, as said, the practical implications follow from lines of thinking, not from ideas and recipes regarding the use of technique or from other forms of practical good advice.

My view is thus that one needs to approach the practical interview work more indirectly and in a more 'reflective' way than is often suggested. To start with the planning and carrying out of interview work and only afterwards enter issues around interpretation of results may appear logical and practical. But we should perhaps not think in such a linear way. It is far better if planning and the carrying out of a study is informed by awareness of the complexity of the interview situation and if practical work is guided by on-going considerations of interpretation. The latter should thus not be reserved for the phase when the empirical material (interview transcripts) lay there on the table in the form of perhaps several hundred pages of texts. This may be too late. Rather than mainly relying on the well structured interview guideline and technical correct acting in the interview (neo-positivistic neutrality or romantic empathy and rapport opening up interviewees), the researcher should be prepared to interpret what goes on in the interview situation and try to deal with unwanted ingredients in this. Such an interpretive orientation has practical consequences, but these need to be determined based on a broader thinking of the interview. It is thus something else than a set of recipes and good advice for the technical and practical conduct of the interview. My point is thus that interpretation of empirical material needs to be conducted on an ongoing basis, even if there is an interchange and switch of emphasis between planning, specific interview activity and post-interviewing desk work during different phases of the research process.

Even though I suggest that the theoretical understanding and the encouragement of multi-faceted interpretation of the interview situation and the responses produced there are most important to illuminate in a method book, and that practical considerations and technical issues are best learned in practice (and to some extent in informal talks with colleagues in the pub), there is still a point in addressing these issues in this book. They are important, but can be dealt with in a concentrated way in the text form. I will below supplement the major orientation of the book with a few brief sections on the planning and conduct of interviews. As said, there is no shortage of literature to consult for the person wanting to read much more about these issues.

The research process

On the purpose with the interview

What the researcher (student, investigator) wants to develop knowledge about is of course crucial for the design of the study. A review of previous studies and theoretical ideas provide clues for what is still not investigated well – or needs to be re-visited. Other studies may be old, weak or be grounded in problematic perspectives. Looking at available studies also gives support in terms of assessments of a possible scope and focus in a new study, as they give clues for what can be reasonably accomplished. It is common to exaggerate what can be produced in a specific study. Things take longer time than expected and interviewees may not that quickly or easily offer as much rich or relevant material as the researcher had hoped for. It is important to reduce the scope of the specific study from a broad interest to a manageable focus leading to an inquiry saying something about some aspects of this broader interest. A lot of what is interesting and important needs to be selected away. It is important to resist the temptation to include too much in a single study like a PhD project.

A problem here is the balancing between an initially broader and more open approach and the need of not too late in the study specify the focus. A risk of failure is to persist in being broad and open for too long, another is to proceed from and maintain a research question that is unproductive – too narrow, or based on an odd concept or an assumption that is taken for granted and not critically reflected upon. Sometimes it is necessary at a later stage in the research process to rethink one's point of departure and framework. A bad research question needs to be reformulated. Expected phenomena may not be that salient or visible or being too elusive to be expressed well in interviews by those one wants to study. Or you may arrive to the insight that your own prejudices, mass media, existing studies or the first people interviewed simply mislead you.

These problems are not possible to entirely eliminate. It is important to continuously question your own ideas and expectations, read the literature critically and try to find a balance between keeping a line and being open and willing to revise research questions and interpretations. An often valuable principle is to initially be more open and broader and then delimit and focus the study. It is important to not do the latter too early, or too late for that matter. (The reader may not find this 'advice' very helpful, but so is the case with a lot of advice.)

It is sometimes the case that it is not until the empirical study is finished (at least the researcher believed was the case) that the researcher has enough knowledge to be able to define and specify what s/he has really studied or would like to study. Sometimes reinterpretation of the empirical material is helpful for getting it all together, sometimes additional empirical material is needed. In the worst case, supplementary work calls for a significant effort, both in terms of rethinking matters and then doing the empirical work.

The purpose of a study is not something that is given once and for all at an early stage of the research process. Initial direction is of course important but interview studies, as all qualitative research, are very much about being open and flexible. More realistic or novel purposes and research questions than the initial often come up over time during a research process. Sometimes the specific purpose is decided fairly late, even in the end rather than the beginning, but this can be risky.

Choice of interviewees

Another key theme is who the lucky ones are to be interviewed. This is of course dependent on the purpose and is in some cases obvious. If the researcher is interested in serial killers, Nobel Laureates in literature or soldiers from the Second World War there are not so many to choose between. In most other cases it is not self-evident who to choose as suitable interviewees.

Sometimes it is difficult to not just identify but to access interview persons. Victims of domestic violence, people nurturing dying family members or people with racist attitudes, may not only be difficult to locate but also unwilling to participate in an interview study. I will here mainly deal with the choices of interviewees as a design issue, in practice often the researcher may need to be satisfied with a sample that is not optimal as practical considerations such as access difficulties, time constraints and geographical distance are important parts of the research process.

In many studies some form of a collective entity (system level) is central. The qualitative researcher then concentrates on one or a few cases with the aim of developing deep, varied and rich knowledge about this or these, either as an end in itself or as a step on the path to a theoretical contribution made possible by the case research. One may want to find something that is representative in one or several respects or one may want to find something that is extreme. 'Extreme' may be in terms of success, problems, history, circumstances, etc. If one for example wants to study social care/therapeutic teams in schools one can identify a school that is having major problems or one with 'average' problems, according to available statistics or informed judgements by experts. Or it is possible to choose team or work according to various criteria: turnover, experience of personnel, reputation for doing good work or whatever.

A case does not have to be a specific social unit, like a school or a work team, but can be a problem case. One possibility is to, within a particular school, find some examples of students with problems and follow these over time or do a concentrated study of those involved and get their observations, experiences, feelings, reflections and so on through a set of interviews. The point here – as we are focusing on the social (or systematic) level – is not to single out the individual identified as having problems as such, but to use him/her as a focal point for understanding student social care/therapy as an institution and as social practice. One can even neglect the individual as such and see how he/she is constructed by a variety of experts and others involved (social worker, psychologist, nurse, parents, teachers, other students, etc.) and investigate problem discussion and decision making of the professionals involved.

In other studies individuals (rather than system level phenomena) are central; they can be studied as rich cases or as a sample indicating a broader group. The unique individual can be more or less interesting for the researcher. One extreme is to see knowledge of a specific case or a set of cases as a partial goal in itself; here rich description of the person is vital. Another is to use individual interviewees solely for instrumental purposes: interview material is then used to produce knowledge of a broader social category, like a social group (female accountants, Facebook users, coffee drinkers at Starbucks) and any of the interviewees are seen as representatives of a broader pattern. In some cases of social entities – like an organization, a political party or a village – key individuals (leaders, whistle blowers) can be important to study, as their work and the organization or village may stand in a close relationship.

When choosing interview persons and deciding on the emphasis put on their accounts there are two major principles. One is *representativeness* in one or another sense, it is important to have breadth and variation among interviewees so that they allow the covering of the social category one aims to address. A holistic coverage and avoidance of bias in the selection of voices of the group being studied is vital. The other principle is to aim for *quality* in the interview responses. The ambition is then to select and/or pay considerable attention to what is assessed to be rich, perceptive and insightful accounts. Here one is less worried about representation and bias and more eager to use the resources – intellectual, verbal, moral commitment to the research project – of highly qualified people with the 'right' experiences and an ability and willingness to communicate these. Sometimes people assessed to have the wanted experiences are key informants and the researcher may cultivate a specific relationship with these persons. They may be targeted for repeat interviews, for advice on who to interview, for help in getting additional background material and for analytical support for a broader understanding of the cultural context at hand. With very qualified interviewees their accounts may be fewer responses to semi-structured interview schedules than self-chosen accounts where the interviewee uses his or her judgement for what to bring forward, as assessed to be helpful for the research project. It is sometimes a bit misleading to talk about interviewees in such cases; informant may be a better term.

Quality-selected interviewees are often helpful as they give much information and provide good material for quotes. Even if the researcher does not consciously aim for selecting and prioritizing a limited number of interviewees assessed to have a lot of value to say, it is common in qualitative research that a small group of interviewees is strongly overrepresented in the interview material visible in the final research publication, at least in studies outside the neo-positivistic pole of the spectrum for qualitative research. Clearly formulated interview statements that seem to be insightful offer good material for citation. There is a risk that interviewees offering such statements too strongly put imprint on the research and that the resulting text give a rather selective, perhaps even biased view of the phenomenon addressed. Not only normal mortals, but also researchers may be tempted to put a lot of faith in people that give an authoritative impression and have rhetorical skills. Sometimes researchers, like people in general, are inclined to rely heavily on individuals that they get good contact with and are similar to themselves in terms of values or other characteristics. In the worst case the researcher and the interviewees whose voices are most well represented in the text share the same prejudices.

In most cases it may therefore be a good idea to combine representation and quality-sampling in the design, e.g. getting some broad representation, but also try to find some interviewees that have much to offer in terms of overview, experiences, interpretations and reflections. Snowball sampling is one possibility here: one can ask interviewees to suggest people that are especially worthwhile to talk to. In terms of the emphasis in using interview material from different people it is generally a good idea to try to get a balance between representation and reliance on 'high-quality' interview material. This means that a variety of voices are respected in analysis and are expressed in the final text, but that this also bears imprints of a strong reliance of interview accounts that are especially insightful or revealing. This typically means that some interviewees receive much more attention and are allowed more voice in the analysis and publication than others. Of course, a certain emphasis on some interviewees does not mean that the researcher accepts what they say without good reason and critical scrutiny. It is important to think through carefully why certain interviewees should be privileged as informants or truth tellers (communicators of superior insights). Also a possible bias of the researcher in the process calls for scrutiny. The researcher needs to use good judgement and consider carefully whether there may be, for example, political interests behind an interviewee's willingness to offer much material or if a capacity as a good storyteller with strong rhetorical skills is mistaken for an ability to provide accurate descriptions. Such use of judgement is – as will be demonstrated in this book's chapters – generally important, but even more so before the researcher puts a lot of trust in a few interviewees delivering a disproportionately large part of the material receiving weight in analysis and represented in the published text. Accounts from key informants need to be backed up with other material. In this book I will discuss these issues at some length.

In some cases, one can choose to pay more attention to certain people because they provide other material than insightful accounts positively helping the researcher to interesting results: interviewees may offer very good examples on something constraining or negative; they may be caught in gender role traps, strongly normalized by discourses on professionalism, political correctness or consumerism or having racist ideas. Here it may be the lack of insightfulness that triggers the researcher. Also here it is of course important to have good reasons for paying much more attention to some cases than others.

Interview guide

Interview studies include a range of versions from highly structured ones, following rather detailed interview guides (so called speaking questionnaires) to rather loosely or even almost non-structured, free and open conversations. The view on research and the specific purpose of studies are of course decisive for the degree of structure in the planning and conduct of interviews. Neo-positivism typically implies a high degree of structure, while romanticism favours semi- or loosely structured interviews.

A high degree of structure reinforces the chances of interviewees responding to rather specific and clear expectations of the researcher (and prevents interviewees from spending the time with talk of less relevance for the researcher's purpose). It also has advantages in that it facilitates the sorting, comparing and analysis of the material. A high degree of structure calls for a clear idea of what kinds of results that one is after, so a lot of thinking through of the project and extensive preparation is called for in order to specify and fine-tune the right questions to ask. Here the reading of existing empirical studies and theoretical work within the research area is called for, although not so much as in questionnaire research (where badly formulated questions can ruin the entire study). The disadvantage of highly structured studies is that they seldom offer that much of really new, interesting and rich results. They tend to answer given questions, not stimulate the raising of new ones.

A low degree of structure means that it is easier to encounter new and unexpected views as the interviewer can use a broad range of the ideas, experiences and observations of those being studied (who are not that much constrained by a rigid set of questions to stick to). The risk – indeed a likely outcome – is of course that interviewees pull in different directions, and that too much interview time is spent letting people talk very freely and associate in different, and sometimes for the research, irrelevant and unproductive directions. The empirical results can be quite dispersed and it may be difficult to hone in and compare the various interview statements. The sorting, comparing and analysis of the material may be difficult and time-consuming and the researcher may have difficulties in writing a convincing method section, where the ways the material has been administered and analysed can be hard to account for. Often loosely or semi-structured qualitative research call for a good deal of intuition and hermeneutic readings and they can't easily be summarized in terms of steps and procedures.

In qualitative studies of the type that is viewed as interesting and is in the focus for this book – being quite far from strongly neo-positivistic research using interviews as speaking questionnaires – it is mainly a question of using some form of semi-structured interview. This means that there are themes to be covered, but in a relatively broad and flexible way. Considerable space is provided for interviewees to bring up what they see as relevant and for the deeper explorations. Interesting emerging themes can call for the sacrifice of obtaining responses to all the questions prepared by the researcher. The questions are typically relatively few and relatively open, sometimes the researcher tries with different questions or language use in order to try to find out what works.

It is of course possible to combine different design elements or tactics in a study in terms of questions with different degrees of structure. One option is to start with a more open and semi-or non-structured sets of interviews in order to learn about the studied group and then get ideas for what, more precisely, to study and perhaps also how to do it. After this exploratory phase the researcher can produce a more specific set of questions to be covered. This is similar to some combined qualitative–quantitative approaches where an exploratory stage is followed by a hypothesis testing or broadly descriptive (quantitative) study. One can also follow a reverse logic: start with a set of highly structured questions and when the results of the interviews are available and analysed, choose some themes for a more rich description, focused exploration and/or deeper understanding through in-depth interviews. These can then have a clear theme and fairly limited focus, but within that frame be quite loose in terms of structure. The idea is then first to get a good description giving a solid basis for the, in a later stage, specifically chosen themes to be explored. A specific set of questions can also be used in order to try to deal with remaining unclarities and to offer more solid material on difficult or controversial issues.

One and the same study can thus use different interview guides, in different stages of the project or with different people, e.g. with one aimed for everybody and then another used with a limited number of key informants, perhaps chosen from the first round or based on the expectation that they have a position or qualities making them suitable for providing more explanatory answers, e.g. a study of workers or professionals can include interviews with union or professional association leaders that presumably can offer some complementary observations and insights in addition to one's findings based on a broad sample of 'ordinary' workers and members of the profession. In particular, in case studies the researcher may vary the kind of questions asked considerably in order to capture different aspects of the case study object, partly to get to the different viewpoints of different interviewees, partly as a result of a gradually emerging understanding of the case, meaning that when certain topics or aspects have been understood it is time not to repeat questions that mainly lead to results confirming what one already knows, but to move on and follow new leads or go deeper into the exploration of themes one has a basic understanding of. In extreme cases the researcher uses several different interview guides – more or less detailed – in the research project.

Interview practice

In the highly structured interview, the idea is that the interview will do a lot of the work and reduce the complexity of the interviewer's task. Sometimes less qualified persons can do the interviewing. As with questionnaire studies, a lot of the thinking needs to be done before the 'data collection' starts. The latter involves more leg work. In other – and often more interesting – interview contexts the interviewer needs to work considerably harder during the interview work. The interaction is much more demanding and calls for consistent use of judgement and interpretation of what goes on and what to do next. It is therefore typically misleading to talk about 'data collection', as if the job is just a matter of going out and tapping people on information. The interviewer needs to think about what are the expectations and thinking of the interviewee, how does he/she interpret and respond to questions, are responses sufficiently clear (in the situation or perhaps they can be expected to be clear(er) when the interviewer reads the notes or the transcripts), are certain themes coming up of sufficient interest to motivate further exploration or should these be dropped in order to not risk wasting valuable interview (and perhaps – later – transcription) time? The interviewer needs to have a good grasp over the entire interview situation as well as the details of what is being talked about at a particular moment. Intensive interpretation is called for and it is not surprising that many interviewers feel tired or even exhausted after a few hours of (semi- or loosely structured) interviewing. Some people claim that they can only do three interviews per day.

Often interview work is divided into a beginning, a middle and an end. Initially the interviewer tries to establish a collaborate relation. The interviewee is being warmed up. This is of course most crucial and perhaps most time-demanding for the romantic researcher while the neo-postivist thinks that less is needed in this respect. Irrespective of the degree of emphasis on warming up interviewees, certain information is provided about the research project and the interviewer, e.g. about background, purpose, status and possible applications and benefits (for society or a group of people). Neutral questions also contribute to create a background for the more explorative or penetrating middle (and substantive) part of the interview.

Here, the idea is to get responses to the questions introduced by the interviewer. He or she perhaps starts with a well demarcated theme and then, when motivated, asks follow-up questions intended to get clarification, increased depth, precision, illustrative examples and verification/support for the interviewee's initial claims. If the interviewer wants to extract the interviewee on more accounts and the latter does not initially respond there are a variety of tricks to use: the interviewer can simply pause (indicating that further talk of the interviewee is expected and appropriate), ask explicitly for more information ('Very interesting, can you say a bit more ...?'), reformulate what the interviewee has said ('Do I understand you correctly if I would express it like ...?'), ask for examples illustrating the interviewee's claims, ask for counter-examples ('Is it sometimes different from how you now describe it ...?'), point at contradictions or introduce doubts ('I have heard other people indicating that the opposite may be the case, namely that ...?'). And so on.

Finally, the interviewer typically asks if the interviewee wants to add something, either supplement earlier talk or introduce something that is relevant but has not really been addressed earlier in the interview: ideas, reflections, suggestions for further work. It happens that when the tape-recorder – if such is used – is switched off, the interviewee talks differently, perhaps less cautiously. This does not necessarily mean that the talk is more truthful or honest, it can be an effect of the interviewer wanting to supplement or balance the earlier talk or that a slight change of the situation means that the interviewer simply feels inclined to talk a bit differently.

Sometimes the interviewer may spend some time and energy in mobilizing the interviewee as an adviser for the remaining part of the research project. Suggestions for new or varied themes for exploration, data sources (revealing events, documents, statistics) or suitable people to interview (e.g. those with a lot of experience, people that are very vocal, that are known to express a different view from the majority of people or seen as intelligent and thoughtful). Using interviewees for finding other interviewees is referred to as snowball sampling.

It happens that the interviewer wants to make a repeat interview with a person and wants to make an agreement about this or just wants to make the interviewee committed to a possible follow-up talk. The final part of the interview can be used for this purpose. Sometimes a follow up can be made over the telephone or Skype, or through email in order to save time. With good contact and confidence this may be sufficient, unless it is a matter of sensitive issues. A first interview by telephone is seldom to recommend, at least not when the purpose (as I have in mind in this book) is to do a fairly rich and deep study. When relevant and possible, a follow-up interview on the phone or Skype is perhaps more successful if it takes place relatively soon after a direct ('body-to-body') interview, as waiting months with the follow up may mean that the contact established will wane. Finally, it is good if the rounding off of the interview is done in such a way that the interviewee feels appreciated as important and is positive to the researcher and project. But this is perhaps self evident and there is no need to say more about this.

A popular question for newcomers to the field of interviews concerns the use of a tape-recorder (or similar instrument) in the interview. Pros and cons are obvious, as is advice about getting acquainted with the equipment and have the batteries loaded, ask the interviewee if he/she objects to the recording of the talk, mention that it can be switched off if/when more sensitive issues are being addressed. One possibility is to record some interviews and refrain from recording in others and instead take notes during and after the interview. The two interview practices can then be compared in terms of various key aspects:

- quality and richness in terms of the responses documented (here recording means that fuller and more exact responses are documented and can be used)
- the interviewer's capacity to think, ask the right questions (that may be negatively affected by the interviewer being distracted by making notes all the time)
- the degree of openness/caution in interviewee responses (recording may mean that interviewees are less inclined to reveal sensitive material).

The interviewer then has good material for making assessments of the gains and losses following from recording respectively note-taking the interview.

What works best is difficult to predict from the start. The sensitivity of interviewees for recording the interviews can vary, partly depending on how safe they experience the relationship with the interviewer and the project. With increasing confidence and knowledge the interviewer may be better in writing down what the interviewee says and think about what questions to raise or follow up at the same time. Over time in the project the interviewer may also improve in terms of making the interviewees feel relaxed and free to respond without worrying about the conversations being recorded – the interviewer becomes better to interact with the group being studied, can refer (anonymously) to what other people have revealed and thereby reduce the uncertainty of interviewees of what may be appropriate to tell in an interview. Development in a research project can thus motivate both increased use or non-use of the recorder, depending on how the researcher can learn over time in dealing with the interview situation.

The researcher needs also to consider the time it takes to transcribe interviews and appreciate that note-taking during interviews can save time and reduce the perhaps more boring parts of the research work.

In between interviews

It is often wise to think through the project between interviews, in the beginning perhaps even after each interview, but even more carefully so between different sets of interviews. So is the case both in terms of the technical aspects – what works and what does not, how can introductions, questions, tactics, etc. be improved? – and in terms of the overall research question and specific themes of study, which can be in need of critical scrutiny and revision or simply be made more precise, alternatively opened up and broadened.

Sometimes the interview work can be divided up in different parts or sequences and the interviewer conduct a preliminary analysis of material from an earlier part or sequence before proceeding with the next. In particular, in case studies it is very important to learn gradually during the process and later stages need to build on, not just add to, what knowledge the interviewer has gained previously in the project. Reading literature during the process – in particular, if preliminary results appear to trigger new and unexpected ideas or paths – may also be motivated. Qualitative research – with the more conservative parts of neo-positivism as an exception – is very much an on-going learning process, where the curious researcher is open about what seems to characterize the area or topic under study. He/she needs to be prepared to revise convictions and plans and make sure that he/she learns not only after but during the work with producing the empirical material (through the interviews and in other ways). Flexibility and improvisation are important here. Through using a conducted set of interviews also as an inspiration for a re-look at the literature and perhaps expanding the reading before doing more interviews there are good opportunities for insight accumulation during the entire process. Of course, much of the learning and production of results come from looking deeply and systematically at all the available material, but to first do all empirical work and then only afterwards start to analyse it may be unfortunate. The very unlucky researcher may then find out very late that some of the assumptions underpinning the study and questions asked were misleading or unproductive. In the worst case, large parts of the work may need to be re-done.

At the same time, it may be difficult due to practical considerations to do a lot of analysis and readings of literature during the fieldwork phase. Sometimes travelling is involved and then doing many interviews in a concentrated way is beneficial. And the interviewer may feel disoriented if unable to concentrate on interview work over a longer period. It can also be a problem if the interviews vary too much, as categorizations and comparisons can be difficult. Qualitative research of the truely 'qualitative type' (acknowledging the complexity of meaning and variations in social life) easily becomes spraggly, and the need for finding and keeping a line of study and a focus is vital, so some discipline domesticating inclinations to spread interview themes and follow any new hunch is a part of the navigation of the entire research process.

Transcripts

In principle, detailed transcript of all taped (or in other ways recorded) interviews is optimal. This makes interpretation work more precisely and easier in some ways and means that exact quotations can be presented. Against this the enormous time involved must be considered, both for transcription and for reading and sorting the material. An average interview-based PhD thesis is perhaps based on 50 interviews and may lead to many hundred, perhaps a thousand pages of interview transcripts. This may imply that the number of interviews that can be carried out must be significantly restricted compared to if the responses are written down (as far as possible) by the interviewer during and after the interviews. A compromise is that the interviewer transcribes those parts of the interviews that are assessed to be most significant and/or does thematic transcribing, i.e. summarizes the major content of what is being said, perhaps indicating where the potentially important parts easily can be found if there is a need for a more precise look at the specific accounts providing details and nuances on a specific theme. The risk is that the interviewer fails to consider quite a lot of what may be interesting and is too much guided by pre-existing ideas or jump to conclusions without carefully having looked at and interpreted the interview material.

The view on transcripts varies between different schools. Neo-positivists seldom pay that much attention to nuances of the language use of interviews while localists see this as the most significant element and have a large apparatus of rules and techniques for the precise transcription of talk. This is almost a science in itself (e.g. Silverman, 2006). Romanticists are often somewhere in between in this respect.

Analysis

The most decisive and demanding work effort is to categorize, interpret and creatively use the interview material. This is possibly in competition with the production of the publication, clearly involving much more than just writing up the results (in particular so in qualitative studies), but this is beyond the scope of this book.

Method authors often emphasize the systematic work with codifying and categorizing interview accounts. Through diligent sortation and categorization work the researcher gets the overview and order of the material and a lot of help in finding patterns and producing results. According to a popular approach such as grounded theory, this leads to theoretical results that are firmly empirically grounded and rigorous (Glaser and Strauss, 1967; Strauss and Corbin, 1994). I am less convinced that the careful and detailed sorting, codification and categorizing interview accounts is always the best way of producing interesting research results. It is grounded in a strong faith that interview accounts offer a solid ground for knowledge development and that correct data management is crucial for good results. As will be shown in this book, this (empiricist) assumption is problematic. Interview material needs to be carefully and critically assessed, not more or less automatically be used as a solid building block for knowledge production. Emphasis on procedures and diligent and detailed work with sorting and categorization easily leads to the research being caught in this potentially time and energy consuming activity at the expense of creative and critical thinking. See Alvesson and Sköldberg (2009) for a critical discussion. As will be clear in this present book there are very strong reasons to take seriously the question what interview material really means and for what purposes it can be used. Only because people in interviews produce certain accounts are there no self-evident reasons why these should be treated as data providing us with strong and reliable indicators on something characterizing social reality or the world views of people outside the interview situation. Interview accounts may not necessarily be seen as mirroring or even indicating the interview persons' experiences, thinking, feelings or values either.

Qualified interpretation work, in which critical questioning and reflection are basic ingredients, is necessary for the use of interview studies being something else and more than ambitious journalism. It also means that research goes beyond data management and sorting, with its empiricist leaning. This means that the principle direction becomes quite different from the sorting, codification and categorization paradigm dominating the mainstream in interview based research (and qualitative research in general, for that matter). What this means is addressed in depth in this book, in particular in Chapter 5 and subsequent chapters.

Final words

As mentioned in the introduction to this chapter, the technical and practical aspects of interview studies are very important, but are on the whole better addressed in specific practical situations than in method texts. It is difficult to give general viewpoints that are highly relevant for the specific acting in interview situations, type somewhat trivial advice such as establish contact, try to create confidence, don't use tape recorder if it makes the interviewee feel uncomfortable, avoid leading questions, ask for clarification when you don't understand, etc. I therefore only provide a fairly brief and concentrated overview of some themes with direct relevance for the practice of interview work. On the whole, interview practice is best supported by a qualified, theoretically thought through understanding, while issues around techniques, procedures and the dealing with practical issues in the field call for less emphasis in a fairly advanced method book such as the present one.

As said in the beginning of this book, the aim here is to offer an alternative to a technically oriented mainstream on interview method, focusing on 'data collection' and 'data management'. I don't see procedures around data collection and processing as the key ingredient in good research. Interview accounts are not without very good reasons to be made into solid building blocks for the carrying out of rigorous research through the careful processing of these. Instead all interview material calls for critical interpretation and rather sophisticated ideas supporting such interpretations. These ideas also have considerable practical implications. I will return to these, but first I will address the need for thinking carefully about how to understand interview situations.

4

A METAPHOR APPROACH

Metaphors have been the subject of increasing attention in recent years, both in social science in general and organizational analysis in particular. They are seen as important organizing devices in thinking and talking about complex phenomena. We never relate to objective reality 'as such' but always do so through forming metaphors or images of the phenomenon we address; organizations are for example seen as if they are machines, organisms, political arenas, brains, theatres, psychic prisons, etc. Families can be seen as consumption units, emotional arenas, reproduction mechanisms or as playgrounds for neurotic interactions. Societies can be viewed as contracts, repression mechanisms, communities, and so on.

Previously it was common to think, and many people still do, that whereas metaphors were useful and necessary in poetry and rhetoric, the precision of science demanded literal expressions and well-defined words (e.g. Pinder & Bourgeois, 1982). Tsoukas (1991) refers to this as the 'metaphors-as-dispensable literary devices' perspective. More commonly, however, metaphors are recognized as vital for understanding thinking and language use in general and as a necessary element in creativity and the development of new approaches to research objects.

A metaphor is created when a term (sometimes referred to as 'modifier') is transferred from one system or level of meaning to another (the principle subject), thereby illuminating central aspects of the latter and shadowing others. A metaphor allows an object to be perceived and understood from the viewpoint of another object. It thus creates a departure from literal meaning: 'a word receives a metaphorical meaning in specific contexts within which they are opposed to other words taken literally; this shift in meaning results mainly from a clash between literal meanings, which excludes literal use of the word in question' (Ricoeur, 1978: 138). A good metaphor depends on an appropriate mix of similarity and difference between the transferred word and the focal one. Where there is too much or too little similarity or difference, the point may not be understood.

A key characteristic of metaphors is that they call for some goodwill, imagination and knowledge of the subject matter. A metaphor, building on the mixing of two elements, means a crossing or carrying over of a concept or idea from one field to another. It is the interaction between the two elements that is of interest and in order for this to work the metaphor user (either as a producer/analyst or a consumer/reader) must emphasize the 'right' aspect of what is carried over as well as what is focused on in the object to be illuminated. Without that the metaphor becomes pointless and frequently absurd. In the pyramid/organization case, the metaphor presupposes a neglect of some of the more robust features of a pyramid, e.g. the amount of stone and technical details of the build, and many significant aspects of social relations in organizations, including fluctuations in relations, feelings, activities, language use and social variation.

In a narrow, traditional sense, a metaphor is simply an *illustrative device*; thus words that make language richer or more felicitous. Metaphors in this sense are often helpful and nice, having a pedagogical and aesthetic value, but are also not crucial and do not structure thinking. A researcher (or any other person) can in principle choose whether to use these metaphors or not.

But metaphors may also be seen as something more profound. In a very broad and basic sense, some people would argue, in contrast to the illustrative device-view all knowledge is metaphorical in that it emerges from or is 'constructed' from some point of view. So, too, are our experiences, for 'our ordinary conceptual system, in terms of which we both think and act, is fundamentally metaphorical in nature' (Lakoff & Johnson, 1980: 3). Metaphors can thus be seen as *crucial elements in how people relate to reality*. Metaphors are, Morgan (1986: 12) says, 'a way of seeing and a way of thinking'. He here refers to 'root metaphors' or organizing metaphors, i.e. metaphors that have a deeper cognitive meaning and that aid and organize our thinking.

Brown (1976) shows that metaphors involve what Aristotle called 'giving the thing a name that belongs to something else'. If a metaphor is taken literally, it will usually appear absurd. The necessary ingredient of difference has a specific cognitive function: 'it makes us stop in our tracks and examine it. It offers us a new awareness' (p. 173). Metaphors are intended to be understood; 'they are category errors with a purpose, linguistic madness with a method' (p. 173). Metaphors must be approached and understood as if they were true while at the same time we are aware that they are fictitious – created and artificial.

All thinking about complex phenomena is based on metaphors (Brown, 1977; Morgan, 1980).[1] As Morgan (1996: 228) writes, our use of metaphor is 'a primal, generative process that is fundamental to the creation of human understanding and meaning in all aspects of life'. Metaphors – in the sense of root or organizing images or gestalts rather than poetic language use – draw attention to implicit aspects and may function as powerful starting points for new ways of seeing. Metaphors may be used in order to provide overviews of intellectual fields and indicate what is illuminated and what is hidden in different perspectives and vocabularies (Gabriel & Lang, 1995; Morgan, 1980, 1997).

Debates and assessments of taking metaphors seriously

The idea of metaphors as a central element in social science (and perhaps in all science) has created a lot of debate. Not everyone applauds the development. From a traditional scientific point of view, the problem with metaphors is that they cannot be translated into more precise, objective language and thus elude rigorous measurement and testing. As Sennett (1980: 78) puts it, 'a metaphor creates a meaning greater than the sum of its parts, because the parts interact'. The metaphorical usage of words involves fantasy and associations that bring with them generative power but limit their appropriateness for empiricists. Pinder and Bourgeois admit that metaphors and tropes cannot be avoided altogether but worry about their uncontrolled, even deliberate use in formal theory:

> In short, because of the impossibility of avoiding metaphors and other tropes in everyday language, they are bound to play a role in the early stages of inquiry, guiding speculations in a heuristic manner. But the ideal of scientific precision is literal language, so, to the extent that it is possible, administrative science must strive to control figurative terms in the development of formal hypothesis and theory. The point at which a trope loses its heuristic value and starts to mislead research and theory construction is difficult to determine. Therefore, it is important to formulate concepts in literal terms that are rooted in observable organizational phenomena as soon as possible during the development of ideas into theory. (1982: 647)

The 'free' use of metaphors means that there is no strict theoretical definition of what is being studied and that it is impossible to establish a good fit between the metaphor and the data, thus making evaluations based on empirical study impossible critics say. This argument proceeds, however, from the assumption that 'objective reality' can be perceived and evaluated as such or on its own terms, i.e. without a gestalt or image standing between the reality out there to be understood and the researcher (or any knowledge-seeker outside academia) trying to make sense of what is going on. In other words, the idea is that we access reality more or less directly and that data give an authoritative basis for assessments and theory. But if, as has been pointed out, all perception is guided by a conceptualization of the object through a gestalt created by metaphorical thinking; it is impossible to let the 'objective data' speak for themselves (Brown, 1976; Morgan, 1983). According to Brown (1976: 178), 'the choice for sociology is not between scientific rigor as against poetic insight. The choice is rather between more or less fruitful metaphors, and between using metaphors or being their victims'.

Even though I would agree with the 'metaphor-fundamentalists' such as Brown and Morgan against the advocates of 'rigor' and hypothesis-testing it is important to recognize a tension between 'scientific rigor' and 'poetic insight'. Even (we) lovers of metaphors must balance creativity and imagination with discipline and carefulness in use of metaphors. Inns and Jones suggest that

> ... metaphor must be used as a rational tool for exploration and be somehow 'literalized' and be made less implicit ... The distinction is that metaphor is used primarily for gestalt understanding in poetry, and essentially for rational reductionist analysis in organization theory. (1996: 115)

They also suggest that while in poetry metaphors and what they evoke may be the *end*, in social science they are mainly *means* for exploration, theory development and empirical analysis. Inns and Jones are, however, aware of the problems of emphasizing the dichotomy between poetry and science and want to soften the clear distinctions somewhat. The ability of metaphors to explore and express experiences for example indicates shared ground between poets and researchers. I would add that careful interpretative work based on the conscious use of a metaphor means an awareness of and tolerance for the ambiguities and tensions involved in the project – something that rigor and rational reductionist analysis will tend to suppress.

A METAPHOR APPROACH

Advantages of thinking in terms of metaphors

The most frequently expressed advantage of metaphors concerns their ability to develop new ideas and guide analysis in novel ways. Mastery of the metaphors involved in thinking and research may thus encourage creativity and provide insight (Grant and Oswick, 1996; Morgan, 1980; Schön, 1979). This is, of course, not only of relevance for academics and others involved in high-brow work, but also for readers of research reports outside academia. This advantage is, as with all developments, to some extent time-bound, as a new metaphor may in one period inspire a rethink of something seen earlier in another way but after some time has passed the new metaphor is then taken for granted and becomes 'frozen'. It also happens, however, that metaphors that have been around for a while may inspire and guide interesting interpretations.

I would also suggest that the development of a new metaphor may in itself be a major part of theoretical progress (a research outcome), i.e. not just an inspiration for it (input to new research). Even though it needs to be explored and guided by as well as guide theoretical and empirical work, it is certainly more than just a conceptual tool to be subordinated to conventional ideas of empirical inquiry.

A second advantage relates to the communicative and pedagogical capacities of metaphors. Metaphors can be used for communicating insights to others, for example as part of the production of scientific texts. People may also use metaphors for expressing their experiences, although the idea here is that it is the cognitive (rather than the poetic) aspect that is crucial. Metaphors thus may facilitate understanding.

A third advantage is that considering metaphors also draws attention to the partiality of the understanding gained by an approach that has been built on a particular root metaphor. As Miles and Huberman (referred to in Inns & Jones, 1996) acknowledged, metaphors work as data-reducing devices. As metaphors so clearly signal (to the metaphor-user and the audience) that the intellectual operation is based on the idea that if we see the phenomenon in a particular, metaphor-guided way, there is an awareness of the partiality and to some extent arbitrariness of the position taken. This facilitates openness and cultivates our tolerance for alternative approaches. Awareness of metaphors and in particular about there being a range of alternative ones may facilitate reflexivity and thus reduce the risk of being caught by one metaphor only.

Difficulties with working with metaphors

Despite the benefits that this use of metaphors appears to offer social research, it also presents some problems. One of these is the risk of using 'bad' ones. One problem here is the temptation to find a rhetorically impressive expression that does not capture the underlying cognition. An appealing metaphor – in the sense of a literal device – may stand in the way of a less elegant but more accurate and elaborate description. This problem basically concerns the level of expression and not so much the root metaphor (and other metaphors guiding thought) itself.

A second problem, once again related to the others, concerns the risk of a supermarket attitude to metaphors (Reed, 1990). There is a chance that focusing on the metaphorical level will draw attention away from the deeper or more basic levels of social research, such as the paradigmatic assumptions on which metaphors rely (on these various levels, see Morgan, 1980). Mastery of a particular perspective demands a complete understanding of its paradigmatic roots and their existential and political aspects. Attempting to employ more than a few guiding concepts in advanced analysis can easily result in superficiality.

A third problem concerns the oversimplifications that can follow, if too much emphasis is put on some elegantly formulated gestalt (metaphor, image) which is seen as guiding and summarizing a line of thinking. It is unlikely that the metaphors employed (espoused) will always illuminate researchers' basic view (gestalt) of the phenomenon. Thinking often can't be captured by (single) words. Complex understanding is perhaps more often derived from a synthesis of different metaphors than from a single sharp-profile picture (Cornelissen & Kaufaros, 2008). This problem arises partly from the limitations of current metaphors and partly from the complexity of the phenomena we deal with. For example, it is unlikely that any researcher sees an organization exclusively as a machine or exclusively as an organism or even exclusively as a combination of the two, or views the consumer as exclusively a hedonist or cultural dope. The addition of further metaphors to 'capture' the framework may simply obscure and distort it; thinking and analysis are not the same as the aggregation of metaphorical bits. There is also the problem that language is being restricted. The words that we have at our disposal do not always adequately signify just what it is we want to pinpoint. They may be elegant and catchy rather than able to aid precision and nuance.

As with almost everything, metaphors are thus not only good or bad but also need to be critically assessed. Researchers working explicitly and ambitiously with metaphors need to be aware of the potential drawbacks in order to use the strengths in order to encourage imagination. In order to facilitate a critical assessment it is important to have access to alternative reference points for (re-) conceptualizing the phenomenon of interest. A set of metaphors is valuable here.

Metaphors in and of research

Let us move on to the area of research and methodology. I will first address metaphors that are frequently used for the entire research project as a whole and/or for empirical work more generally, and then move on to the interview more specifically and the metaphors used for thinking about it (or taking it for granted and thus perhaps not really thinking about it).

General metaphors for research[2]

A predominant image seems to represent research as *mushroom-picking*. (For readers in countries where mushrooms are usually bought in shops, the expression 'berry-picking' may be an alternative!) All talk about the collection of data, the capture of data, the codification and classification of data, and so on, points to a metaphor of this kind. By carefully and painstakingly collecting and sorting through a sufficiently large amount of 'data', the raw materials are acquired to make a delicious dish that can be prepared according to the recipe book (compare 'the processing of data'). As has already become clear, I regard research guided by the mushroom-picking metaphor as unproductive, at least as the main metaphor for research. Empirical material – interview accounts, observations of social situations – should not be reified. The mushroom-picking metaphor might possibly facilitate some of the practical aspects, but it expresses a naïve empirical view and stands in opposition to more reflective research ideals.

Talk of 'data collection' is unfortunately widespread in qualitative methodological contexts. Even interpretive and critical scholars will often use the expression (e.g. Rosen, 1991; Thomas, 1993; Van Maanen, 1995). Sometimes this may be justified by reasons of convenience – other expressions might mean using more words and these becoming unwieldy. And we should also remember that particular metaphorical expressions do not necessarily tell us all that much about what metaphors are used on a cognitive level. I get the feeling that many people do not think of the concept as a metaphor. Certain sections of research may also be clarified or guided reasonably well with the help of this metaphor. Nevertheless, it remains too prevalent, even in research contexts where the demands on awareness and reflection are high. It is not just the innocent use of a word, it has some consequences for the framing of and thinking about the research process.

One analogy, which like the mushroom-picking metaphor seeks to warn us of the pitfalls of traditional, dataistic methodology, invokes certain similarities between this and (early versions of) capitalism:

> In the world of science, as in the world of capitalism, it is a question of playing safe. Intellectual adventurousness is in some obscure way attractive, yet basically reprehensible, just like commercial freebooting. People imagine that life is so organized that all forms of saving – even of scientific data – will grow and yield compound interest. And they will grow on their own. The only thing we have to do is to invest sensibly and then show great restraint. Stock-exchange quotations and significance testing may appear to resemble each other. So-called hard data are sometimes bewilderingly like hard currency. 'Data banks'... (Asplund, 1970: 96; my translation)

Associated with the problems of seeing 'data' as something one 'collects' is the expression of the overall purpose of grounded theory and other data-centric approaches. Advocates of these believe that their aim is to 'discover' or 'build' a theory. The problem is, of course, that a theory must – at least in part – be created: it is not just lying there waiting for a researcher-discoverer to find it, like an explorer discovering a hitherto unknown island (cf. Woolgar, 1983), or for the constructor to use the material as robust building blocks and build the theory.

So much for metaphors that are commonly used but quite problematic as they tend to be taken for granted and underestimate the uncertain nature of empirical material. Using 'anti-metaphors' (metaphors intended to point at negatively loaded meanings) like talking about data collection as mushroom-picking reveals the traps into which empirical research can fall. There are also examples of metaphors being used to seek in a more positive manner to encourage other, more 'interesting' and less 'mechanical' or objectivist views of the research process. For example, Czarniawska-Joerges (1992) uses the phrase 'insight gathering' instead of 'data collection'. Asplund (1970) suggests that the research process can be compared to a detective novel as it is about solving a mystery. Good research contains two central components: formulating the mystery and then solving it (see also Alvesson & Kärreman, 2010, for how this idea can be used in empirical studies). In critical theory, defamiliarization and cultural criticism are possible metaphors for research (Alvesson & Deetz, 2000; Marcus and Fischer, 1986). (Defamiliarization, however, is also used more widely in cultural research.) Postmodernists have suggested some radically different metaphors for qualitative research (or at least certain varieties of it). Thus Clifford (1986: 6) talks about research as 'true fiction', while Brown (1990) refers to research activities as 'rhetorical constructions'. Research is writing or authorship (Richardson, 2000; Van Maanen, 1995).

Certain other researchers cite metaphors that give more space to the social component in research, and in doing so they emphasize the importance of the interview subjects. Steier (1991), for instance, sees social science research as 'co-construction', whereby the researcher in interaction with the research subject constructs the research object. Denzin and Lincoln (2005) also emphasize the variety of elements in research work but use the metaphor 'bricolage' as indicating a more electic, relaxed and playful process. The qualitative researcher is then viewed as a 'bricoleur' or 'maker of quilts', who is using the aesthetic and material tools of craftswork and making use of the various strategies, methods and empirical materials available.

Thus far we have looked at metaphors that can illuminate the research process as a whole, or at least certain important parts of it. But there are also metaphors that can throw light on some more delimited sections or dimensions of the process. 'Hard and soft data' represent a fairly typical case in point. Many researchers emphasize the literary qualities of science and the role of the researcher as author, as well as the poetic elements in texts (e.g. Richardson, 2000). Yet perhaps the most important point to consider with regard to particular sections or dimensions of research concerns the metaphors that are used, more or less consciously, for language. Von Glasersfeld compares two such metaphors:

> Language does not transport pieces of one person's reality into another's – it merely prods and prompts the other to build up conceptual structures which, to this other, seem compatible with the words and actions the speaker or writer has used. (1991: 23)

Language as a means of conveying meaning (a transport vehicle) is thus confronted here by language as inspiration or as building blocks in the construction of concepts (cognitive trigger). Elsewhere I and a co-author have discussed how empirical material – rejecting the metaphor 'data' as this implies a view of interview statements, questionnaire responses, etc. as highly robust and reliable – can be conceptualized in different metaphorical ways (Alvesson & Kärreman, 2010). We criticized the view that empirical material/data is best seen as a judge (making verdicts of what is true or false) or a signpost (showing the way to knowledge). Instead we have suggested that empirical material should be thought of as a critical dialogue partner. The idea is that empirical material must be mobilized to 'say something'. Also the interviewee can, as I will come back to, be viewed as a critical dialogue partner, but my point here is that we must view the empirical material in this way.

Metaphors for the research interview

As I see it, the dominant metaphors for the research interview are 1) an instrument, to be used as effectively as possible in the more or less capable hands of a researcher, and 2) a human encounter, encouraging an interviewee to reveal her authentic experiences. Often these will be combined – the instrument is in the service of messy social engineering rather than surgery and this calls for interaction with a human touch in order for the interview-tool to work. Arguably, these metaphors are pragmatically helpful and fit into neo-positivistic, respectively romantic epistemologies, but draw attention away from significant aspects of the interview as a complex social situation.

However, there are also other ideas on how to indicate views of the interview in terms of metaphors. Kvale (1996) suggests two contrasting metaphors for the interviewer: miner and traveller. These have some overlap with my two metaphors for the situation but there are also differences, as they highlight partly different sets of aspects. In the miner metaphor, 'knowledge is understood as buried metal and the interviewer is a miner who unearths the valuable metal. Some miners seek objective facts to be quantified; others seek nuggets of essential meaning' (1996: 3). The alternative, the traveller metaphor, views interview material as something that is partly formed and transformed by the interviewer-researcher: 'The potentialities of meanings in the original stories are differentiated and unfolded through the traveller's interpretations; the tales are remoulded into new narratives, which are convincing in their aesthetic form and are validated through their impact upon the listeners' (p. 4).

A rather different take on the interview can be found in Schwalbe and Wolkomir (2003) who address interviews with men and see the interview as a struggle for control. They argue that 'men try to exert a sort of compensatory control over the interview situation' (p. 59). This urge for control reflects a prevailing gender order in which hegemonic masculinity means that 'men who wish to claim the full privileges of manhood must distinguish themselves from women by signifying greater desires and capacities for control of people and the world, autonomous thought and action, rational thought and action ... ' (p. 56). In order to live up to and sustain this image and sense of self, male interviewees then seek to minimize vulnerability through control over the interview situation. The interviewer is, however, eager to move beyond the subject's signifying masculinity and to reach deeper experiences and honest accounts. This implies that the interview situation (at least with men as interviewees) becomes a battle for control.

A quite different image of the interview is proposed by Holstein and Gubrium (2003a), seeing interviewees not as difficult people that need to be managed but as knowledge-producers: 'Treating interviewing as a social encounter in which knowledge is constructed means that the interview is more than a simple information-gathering operation: it's a site of, and occasion for, producing knowledge itself' (p. 4).

Are those being interviewed then to be seen as respondents, participants or informants? Or even co-researchers? This is not just a matter of semantics, but the various expressions indicate the different roles and meanings for their contributions. Is what is being told by interviewees seen as 'data', 'accounts', 'stories' or 'talk' – or even as knowledge? These words indicate different possible metaphors, i.e. cognitive understandings. If researchers mean something with metaphors (and do not use words carelessly without any particular intent or idea, i.e. referring to those one talks with as 'informants' for example without considering whether the word communicates something distinct), we can get quite different understandings of what goes on here in terms of what an interviewee does: the person being interviewed as a deliverer of data is something else than a storyteller or conversationalist or a co-constructor of knowledge. Note that the meaning and significance of the last metaphor comes through more strongly in arguments that the good interview should not be about control but empowerment, leading to 'the result then, is more of a team effort, rather than a division of labour, even though the discourse of empowerment still aims to put the narrative ball in the respondent's court, so to speak'

(Holstein & Gubrium, 2003a: 19). There seems to be some confusion of metaphors here; perhaps the interviewee, having the ball so to speak, is, through having been empowered by the researcher, more of a leader than a respondent. (Normally, the person with the ball temporarily directs the game and others must respond.) But the set of metaphors used here – team person, empowerment and narrative ball – on the whole give some backup to the co-constructor of knowledge metaphor. The interviewee comes through as an expert, someone whose insights and knowledge put strong imprints on the research outcome. This is something quite different than the stimuli-driven labourer managed, by the researcher managing the interview schedule, to deliver a set of structured data on request.

The metaphors for the interviewer, the research interview and the interviewee thus vary considerably and sometimes researchers will choose to mix metaphors (as in the case of the empowered team-member respondent, just discussed) thus creating some confusion, which suggests the need for further elaboration and a clarification of how one understands the interviewee.

Conclusion

The point about the (root) metaphors discussed in this chapter is that, at best, they provide a holistic and suggestive picture of the phenomenon that facilitates thought and gives it an overall direction. Metaphor may provide guidance that counteracts the tendency to get caught in the struggle with empirical impressions, which easily leads the researcher to give priority to data management (codification, classification and so on) and thus to fall back on dataistic assumptions. By pointing out a few problematic metaphors – problematic in the sense of reinforcing empiricist assumptions, over-relying on interview statements as 'data' to proceed from (build on) – researchers can acquire some guidelines that may help them to avoid the particular trap in question.

I am not advocating any definite metaphor for research as the best one. But I do feel that the ironic use of the metaphor of mushroom-picking (for 'data collection' work) has some value as a counterweight to the ideas that dominate qualitative (and to an even greater extent quantitative) methodology. That empirical work is much more ambiguous and constructing than is suggested by the expression 'collecting data' (and then discovering or building something based on it) must be taken seriously. Otherwise, I would like to emphasize the value of having access to several different and complementary research metaphors, both for 'negative' (pointing at traps) and 'positive' (aiding interpretation) purposes. Exactly which ones are chosen will depend on what has personal significance for individual researchers or what works generatively for them within the context of specific research projects. The point here is that having access to several different metaphors facilitates offering various comprehensive images of research, thus reducing the risk of latching on to a one-sided and favourite conception.

Having a favourite metaphor is common and reasonable but the trick is to have a certain distance in relation to it – that is, an ability to look at one's favourite position from another angle. Of course, all interview researchers will understand that sometimes reality clashes with one's basic view and calls for an adaption to the unexpected. A researcher seeing the interview as the co-constructing of knowledge will sometimes face situations in which an interviewee simply can't deliver much in the way of helpful descriptions or ideas. Or a researcher seeing the interview as an instrument and expecting an interviewee to straightforwardly deliver data may sometimes have to stop and rethink: an interviewee can be very insightful and communicate much more than mere 'information' or s/he can be so shallow, confused or unreliable that the responses are not trustworthy. But my point is that we should access alternative viewpoints so that we can think in contradiction to our favoured metaphors and not just deviate from the thinking they encourage in those exceptional cases where they clearly don't work. We should be able to think through alternative non-obvious ways of making sense of what takes place in an interview. Metaphors should be chosen in order to stimulate reflection and movement between different lines of interpretation. The next chapter tries to offer a set of metaphors that are helpful in this respect.

Notes

1 A review of the debates on the virtues and problems with emphasizing metaphors can be found in Grant and Oswick (1996).
2 This section draws upon Alvesson & Sköldberg (2009), Chapter 9.

5

RETHINKING INTERVIEWS:
NEW METAPHORS FOR INTERVIEWS

My key argument in this book is that we can't be satisfied with a limited set of assumptions about the research interview informed by one metaphor and then proceed as if this would normally lead to the production or construction of qualified data that we can then use as a solid basis for making interpretations and drawing conclusions. Using the dominant metaphor of the interview as an instrument for data collection gives a partial but narrow support for understanding and working with interviews. The interview as a complex social situation may bear the imprints of a multitude of social logics, mechanisms or social forces that need to be theorized and assessed. This easily means a high level of complexity to consider for the interviewer. A key question is how this can be handled. In this chapter I present a framework for how to think through the interview and thereby aid interpretation and reflexivity. It is based on eight metaphors for the (research) interview. These can be seen as a repertoire of interpretive resources counteracting commonsensical and instrumentalist positions. Formulated a bit more drastically they can be employed as an antidote to naivety. (Whether they work as an antidote to cynicism, hyper-scepticism or paralysis I am less certain, so be aware, dear reader!) By capturing ideas in the form of metaphors I hope that it will be easier to grasp and remember the key points made.

The interview as a complex act: eight problems facing an interviewee

This chapter is based on an effort to think through the complexities of the interview situation in a fundamental way. I am drawing upon a large variety of various philosophical, social and behavioural, theoretical and methodological literatures plus my own experiences as a researcher and as a project leader for rather large qualitative research projects, mainly or partly based on interviews. The choice of eight alternative understandings – alternative that is to the conventional, data-reporting ones – reflects a desire to bring or integrate a wider set of considerations, but without complicating the issues too much. Eight seems the maximum here, offering a set of options from which the practising researcher can pick.

The metaphors suggested below all represent different understandings of interviews and involve a rather basic critique of dominant views on the subject matter. The set of metaphors suggests reconceptualizations with wide ranging implications for interview-based research. Each involves a key feature of an interview and a central problem (challenge) that an interviewee must 'solve' or relate to:

1 The social problem of coping with an interpersonal relation and complex interaction in a non-routine situation.
2 The cognitive problem of finding out what it is all about (beyond the level of the espoused).
3 The identity problem of adapting a self-position which is contextually relevant (and/or comfortable for the interviewee).
4 The 'institutional' problem of adapting to normative pressure and cognitive uncertainty through mimicking standard forms of expression.
5 The problem (or option) of maintaining and increasing self-esteem that emerges in any situation involving examination and calling for a performance (or allowing esteem-enhancement to flourish in the situation).
6 The motivation problem of developing an interest or rationale for active participation in the interview.
7 The representation/construction problem of how to account for complex phenomena through language.
8 The 'autonomy/determinism' 'problem' of a powerful macro-discourse operating behind and on the interview subject.

Table 5.1 provides a summary.

One could of course also add the interview as an instrument and a knowledge-building human encounter as metaphors to the list, but as they are already fairly well understood and my point is to add to the common assumptions about the use of interviews, I am not covering these here. Other metaphors to supplement and challenge the dominating one could of course be considered: the interview as empowerment, therapy, learning experience … . These tend to assume something about

Table 5.1 A summary of the eight metaphors of interviews

Metaphor	Key Problem/Feature	Theory	Neopositivism (Non)response	Romanticism (Non)response	Localism (Non)response
Local accomplishment	The mastering of complex interaction in the interview situation takes precedence	Interpersonal theory, micro-sociology	Denial; minimization of interaction through strict interview procedure	Partial denial; through establishing contact the interviewee relaxes about 'performing'	Acknowledgement of local accomplishment being a key feature of the interview situation
Establishing and perpetuating a storyline	Ambiguity of situation and the problem complex targeted in interview, sense-making leading to development of assumptions	Cognition, sense-making	Clear, carefully structured set of questions reducing the need for the interviewee to try to find out what the researcher is up to	Unclear: one option is to be open and informative about the research projects, another is reducing the space for sense-making through dialogue	Partly outside what localists focus on as it involves speculations about interviewee's interpretations and sense-making work
Identity work	The interview situation calls for and makes possible the adoption and securing of one or several identity positions (multiple selves)	Self-identity, role theory, multiple selves (post-structuralism)	Denial: The structuring of the situation means researcher control over identity or that responses not being based on a particular sense of self	Encouragement of authentic self coming forward, making genuine response possible	Indications of identity work and self-positioning directly tied to the situation is a possible object of study
Cultural script application	Difficulties of representation and normative pressure for adopting certain talk	Discourse theory, institutional theory, critical theory	Denied/minimized: to some extent counteracted through specific questions	Denied: possible to avoid/minimize through interaction bringing genuine forward responses	Acknowledged, a possible object of study

(Cont'd)

Table 5.1 (Cont'd)

Metaphor	Key Problem/Feature	Theory	Neopositivism (Non)response	Romanticism (Non)response	Localism (Non)response
Moral storytelling	An interest in making a good impression, promoting oneself and one's group in moral and rational terms	Culture theory, discourse theory	Denied/minimized: to some extent counteracted through specific questions	Risk reduced due to interview technique aimed at encouraging honesty	Acknowledged but difficult to study as it is hard to sort out 'moral storytelling' from other ingredients
Political action	Interview subjects located on political arenas and driven by interests in promoting certain kinds of truth	Theory on politics and power, critical discourse analysis	Denied/minimized: to some extent counteracted through specific questions	Risk reduced due to interview technique aimed at encouraging honesty	Falls somewhat outside the research agenda of localists as it assumes interests which often can not be induced from the local situation at hand
Construction work	Problems of representation and the ambiguity of language	Discourse theory type Potter & Wetherell	Denied: inconsistent with neo-positivist assumptions	Denied: inconsistent with romantic assumptions	Acknowledged, a possible object of study
A play of the powers of discourse	Interviewees not being integrated actors 'in control' but discursively constituted, responding within and constrained by discourse	Foucault poststructuralism	Denied: inconsistent with neo-positivist assumptions	Denied: inconsistent with romantic assumptions	Falls somewhat outside the research agenda of localists as it assumes macro power, which often can not be induced from the local situation at hand

the outcome of interviews that is often difficult to find something to say about. I think these (except possibly for reflection-stimulation) would mainly be relevant only for rare cases that were related to specific topics. There is little point in extending the list beyond eight as I think these illuminate a wide spectrum of important aspects which are relevant to consider for many, perhaps even most, interviews.

An example: talking hierarchy

In order to show the relevance of the metaphors for understanding empirical material I will use an example and then throughout the chapter apply the various metaphors to it illustrating their usefulness. For this I present a brief excerpt from an interview with a senior consultant in a large IT/management company. The research project was a rather ambitious one, including in total over 50 interviews and some participant observation on a range of aspects of the management consultancy firm, treated as a case study. There is no need here to include more on this. (For details, see for example Alvesson & Kärreman, 2007; Kärreman & Alvesson, 2009). The interviewee is male, mid-30s, has worked for the firm his entire career and is moving up the ladder. He is on parental leave but does not mind coming to the corporate building with the small baby, who sleeps during the entire interview. During the interview he gives an open and relaxed impression. In the interview we talked about a number of themes, including motivation (motives/driving forces for people in the company), as part of a rather open (half-structured/thematic) talk raising questions regarding what characterized the organization and the people working there. I will throughout this section produce interpretations of it based on the various eight metaphors. I will, for space reasons but also as a consequence of not all of the eight metaphors working equally well on this specific material, sometimes be brief.

> I get the impression that most people here are heavily focused on their career. For them it is important to have a good job with high prestige and right promotion. Right at the time when one is thinking that one is prepared or has worked a certain time or something similar. Well ... for me, for me then, hierarchy has a tendency to sound negative, for me hierarchy has certain advantages, including that those above you take care of you to some extent, and that you should take care of those below you. So this is a rather educating environment and that I find good. So to me hierarchy is not negative, but it guarantees quite a lot. Then I am extremely sensitive to when there are wrong individuals on top. How in hell could they get there ...?

From conventional research points of view, the interviewee, although mainly positive to 'hierarchy', show some ambivalence towards it. A neo-positivist may assume that this reflects his attitudes and/or the structure of the company, while a romantic may interpret this is as an expression of the meaning ascribed to hierarchy, an arrangement facilitating care, responsibility, support and personal development, but also dependent on the right people and orientations being in place. As will be seen below, there are other ways in which the account can be understood.

1 The interview in its context: accounts as local accomplishment

An interview is a social situation in which two persons (or more) who are typically unfamiliar to each other will meet for a short period of time, on average around one or two hours. The interviewer will have set up this situation 'in order that the respondent speaks openly, authentically or truthfully, to produce valid reporting on some interior or exterior state of affairs' (Baker, 1997: 130) so that the interviewer can use this speech as 'data' in a research publication. What takes place during the interview may, however, be seen as complex interaction in which the participants will make efforts to produce a particular order, draw upon cultural knowledge to structure the situation, minimize any embarrassments and frustrations, have feelings of asymmetrical relations of status and power, etc.[1] Making the other person comfortable, saving face, making him or her open up and engaging in 'relevant', productive talk through a mix of means, including providing clues for what is interesting and what is not, calls for activity on behalf of the interviewer. There are, as explained in the previous chapter, different opinions in the literature concerning the optimum degree of friendliness *vs* neutrality and interviewer activity *vs* avoiding creating bias through too much interference. The dilemma is a classical one (Cicourel, 1964).

Irrespective of preferences here, a complex social interaction that aims to establish a functioning micro-order takes precedence over the researcher triggering productive responses through certain techniques. An interplay between two people, each with their own gender, age, professional background, personal appearance and ethnicity, puts a heavy imprint on the accounts produced. Parker (2000), for example, noted how age had a strong significance in his interviews with managers: in some cases, with older interviewees, he was addressed as a junior, a novice, while in others, with people around his age, he was used as a

80

confidante, and in a third type of relation, with very junior and/or marginal people, he was seen as an expert (a management consultant or even a management spy). As mentioned in Chapter 2, Jorgenson (1991) – while presenting herself as a communication researcher interested in how families think about family life – was perceived as a research psychologist by some interviewees and as a family expert by others. (As she was visibly pregnant during the last part of the research the position of 'soon-to-be-first-time-parent' also become salient for some interviewees.) As an 'expert' she was more often seen as a potential critic who would evaluate participants' responses with reference to what was normal or appropriate. She argued that 'the person to whom a research subject speaks is not the person an interviewer thinks herself to be' (1991: 211).

More mundane issues, such as physical location, may also matter when framing the interview. Some researchers note different responses when interviewing managers in their offices from other settings (parking area, home, cantina) (Easterby-Smith et al., 1991).[2] The specific words used of the interviewer, his/her gestures, writing behaviour (accounts may be followed by more or less intensive note-taking), and so on affect the responses of the interviewee. Carrying the point on a bit further, Schneider (2000: 162), in a study of interviewing in an educational organization, showed how interviewers were not 'simple conduits for answers but rather are deeply implicated in the production of answers'. Accounts produced are in themselves empirical phenomena calling for explanation, not reflections of other empirical phenomena or 'proofs' for explanations of these, localists would argue (Baker, 1997; Silverman, 2006, etc.).

The significance of the interview as local accomplishment makes it more reasonable to see interview accounts as contingent upon the specific situation and too local to be able to treat as reflections of how the interviewee thinks, feels, talks and acts in other situations that are totally different from the interview situation. The interviewee becomes different persons in different relationships – a person is not the same when interviewed by somebody perceived as a consultant reporting directly to a superior in an organization or as a young person who needs help in order to produce a dissertation. Different identities come forward when we are interviewed by somebody who we perceive to be a research psychologist, a family expert, a communication researcher or a soon-to-be-first-time-parent, to refer to the case of Jorgensen reviewed above. This calls for an appreciation of the local nature of interview talk and the specific identities that can come to the fore in this specific situation – and which may be loosely coupled to the identities that are constituted and expressed in other situations.

In the interview excerpt above (i.e. the management consultant interviewed), from a local accomplishment metaphor the account indicates how the interviewee produces a nuanced view on motivation and hierarchy which is coherent with the situation. Part of this is the interviewer, an academic working at a business school whose appearance (dress code, etc.) indicates little interest in the formal status and whose questions focus on the culture, people and other human interests. It is possible that the interviewee addressing hierarchy in a particular way – taking a nuanced, somewhat ambivalent stance on it and using caring vocabulary – is a response to the specific interpersonal situation in which the account is produced. The interview statement may thus be seen as an outcome of the scene more than as a reflection of the organization 'out there' or the interviewee's mind 'in there'.

2 Framing the situation: the interview as establishing and perpetuating a storyline

In some versions of anthropology and interpretative research more generally, the task of the researcher will be to go out there and find out what subjects think of the study they are involved with. The interviewee may ask him or herself a similar question when this (in most cases) unknown person from a university turns up and expects to have a number of questions answered. How does the interviewee think about the world in terms of social inquiry and doing interviews? The respondent may wonder about the kind of project the researcher is doing: what are they really up to, how are they doing it, and why? The interviewee may be more or less ambitious in her quest to find out what the researcher may be up to but is in most cases also inclined to develop some kind of understanding of what the research project is about and how the results can be used. The interviewee becomes temporarily enrolled in a project of which s/he knows rather little and may rely on guesswork and fantasies about what it is all about. What interviewees think about the situation may vary considerably and differ heavily from what researchers think that they think or would like them to think. As Holstein and Gubrium (2003a) point out, the subject position and voice of the interviewee must be considered in relation to the researcher: 'Who after all, is the interviewer in the eyes of the respondent?' (p. 22).

The assumptions that the interviewee develops in order to be cooperative and competent in the position may far from always become explicit during the interview. Occasionally, however, they will. In a study of blue-collar workers in washing factories, people were asked about their image (cognitions) of these organizations, but answered as if the question concerned their job satisfaction, apparently reflecting the assumption that academics interviewing low-level employees were only interested in job satisfaction and related issues, such as discontent and absence, etc. (Lidström-Widell, 1995). Whyte (1960) described a research project where he tried unsuccessfully to clarify a particular subject with specific questions. It was only after revealing to the interviewee the particular puzzle behind a question that Whyte got the 'right' (i.e. for him, relevant and useful) answer. This example illustrates the significance of behind-the-surface-thinking. The interviewee is not, and cannot be, 'blank'. He/she probably asks him or herself: who is the interviewer? What is he/she up to? What is he/she really after? What may be helpful/interesting for him/her? Does he/she understand this issue and how can I correct any misunderstandings or in other ways influence the shape of the project? As this often is beyond the control of the researcher it does create a problem, but it is also an important resource as the interviewee's framing of what the interview, or a theme within it, is basically about may be necessary in order to produce a relevant account.

Interviewees do not just produce relevant information within specific fields of interest for a research project, but also engage in sense-making activity. The latter is needed for the former to be delivered, unless the interview is not about trivial matters (age, number of children). In qualitative research, at least outside the neo-positivist camp, the purpose is to explore complex, often personal matters, and it is often insufficient to put forward clear questions that can be easily understood and given a standard, context-free meaning. Intensive interpretation of what the researcher is after – before, during, and perhaps after the interview (and before a repeat interview) – and the forming of work assumptions of what the entire exercise is about and how specific themes addressed should be understood to guide interviewee responses.

Neo-positivists would argue that well-structured questions limit the need to take seriously the sense-making activities guiding the answers. Romantics would emphasize the need and possibility to bridge frameworks and to develop a shared 'mini-paradigm' between the active interviewer and the participant-interviewee making possible a co-production of knowledge. The metaphor suggested here assumes that the interview is a highly ambiguous situation calling for intensive sense-making on behalf of the interviewee, making what is espoused an outcome of the interviewee's implicit 'work paradigm' as much as the explicit interventions of the researcher. The complex cognitive activities of the interviewee – to a large extent hidden from the interview – may be of more significance for the accounts produced than the interviewer's explicit input in giving clues for understanding the situation. The latter probably often only plays a minor role: to explain in depth what the study is all about is time-consuming and may also steer the interviewee too much. In addition, what the researcher explains and how the interviewee reads this may deviate considerably. There is thus a black box of interviewee thinking that is not easily accessible for the researcher and this production of assumptions about the research project and the interview may be a major input to the talk produced. Interview responses may be less about direct answers to explicit questions than the interviewees' more or less personal beliefs and fantasies of what this is all about and what seems relevant enough to say, as illustrated by the case of the washing factory workers referred to above.

In the interview example with the senior consultant above, the interviewee may have developed the assumption that organizational structures and career issues are of key interest for management researchers, which makes its understandable that the explicit question on 'motivation' in relation to climbing the ladder leads to talk about the hierarchical structure.

3 Tuning in the subject: the interview as identity work

A basic aspect related to sense-making activities is the identities that are called upon in interview work. These frame the situation and guide responses. No non-trivial account about the organization one works in is produced outside or abstracted from identity, i.e. self-definition and efforts to accomplish a feeling of coherence and direction. Interview work means that the interviewer – and the interviewee – invoke an identity, in explicit and implicit ways. Identities are relational in the sense that how we see ourselves has a situational and social dimension: for example, a person 45 years old probably sees herself as mature when talking with someone 25 and fairly young when interacting with a 65 year old. When thinking in terms of profession and employment, other aspects of self become salient than when the context circles around families and parenthood. (For a review of various understandings of identity, see Alvesson, 2010.)

Identity work may emphasize how a particular sense is expressed in the interview or how it is more actively performed. The latter view typically rejects 'essentializing theories that assume the unity of an inner self' (Riessman, 2003: 337) and suggests that actors in social settings stage performances of their desirable selves that are situated and accomplished in social interactions.

If somebody is interviewed as a 'woman', a 'leader', a 'middle-level manager', different identities are invoked and different inclinations to interpret the entire interview situation, different specific questions and evaluations of what kinds of answers are then appropriate. The work situation and the organizational conditions of a woman, a leader and a middle manager – even if it is the same biological person – are not the same. Of course, often a specific identity will be focused on in a research project (i.e. as a woman in a male world or as a person in the middle trying to balance the demands of superiors and subordinates) so if an interviewee responds accordingly that is fine. At least it will facilitate smooth interaction.

But quite often these identities will not be clearly signalled, neither from the interviewer nor the interviewee, and the researcher may be unaware of how language use and other signals may operate on the person being interviewed in terms of identity. Being explicit about the identity position that is optimal for a research project may be counterproductive as it fixes the responses too firmly. A person addressed as a 'leader' by the researcher may not do 'leadership' that much; an individual identified as a middle manager may not feel that the middle position is that central during everyday life; but in the interview context, prescribed positions may encourage constructions in which 'leadership' and 'middle management' may be salient and the responses will reflect such temporary identity positions. Similarly, a person may not define him or herself as a car driver or a voter as a particular significant aspect of who s/he is and sees her/himself, but may see cars and voting as 'low on meaning/symbolism' and 'outside' self-identity. A researcher may get an interviewee tuned in on a specific identity position, assuming that this captures something central (e.g. the manager as a leader, the professional being oriented towards competence

85

development, the consumer being in favour of sustainable development), but the interviewee may then focus on and emphasize the few marginal situations in which this identity makes sense. The researcher wanting depth and checking that this is not just talk may ask questions about practices but the examples chosen may be less typical and also framed in a specific way.

Frequently researchers will more or less strongly encourage interviewees to adopt certain identities and avoid others. The interview situation will run more smoothly if there is a correspondence between role expectations and the identity construction in the situation. But the interviewee adapting to the role prescription and identity construction inherent in the researcher's framing of the situation and questions asked is not the sole complication. The interviewee may also use the interview situation – in which an empathetic listener is at one's disposal – to express, elaborate, strengthen, defend and/or repair a favoured self-identity. In one sense, the romanticist interviewer strives to come forward by appearing as the interviewee's best friend (during the interview): building up a warm environment, being attentive, listening, supporting, doing everything to build trust and make the other person feel safe enough to reveal thoughts, feelings and fantasies in an authentic way.

But despite the interviewer's intensive efforts and possible success in getting the interviewee to be authentic, it is still not necessarily the 'true self' that will emerge, but what may be seen as an effort to construct a valued, coherent self-image. Fairly open questions – how do you see yourself, what do you do as a parent (voter, worker, motorist, lover …) – may inspire an interviewee to move to a favourable identity position allowing for a construction and expression of an idealized self. In a study of advertising workers, subjects described themselves as intuitive, sensitive, emotional, committed, artistic, serious, but also results-oriented, etc. This can be seen as reporting the truth on how they are or how they coherently see themselves (stable self-images), but perhaps less speculatively on how they present themselves and try to construct an identity in this specific situation, i.e. the interview is a site for situation-specific identity work (Alvesson, 1994). This then does not refer to a fixed and ready identity that is straightforwardly expressed, but instead to efforts to create, reinforce adapt or even patch an identity.

Typically, the interview can be seen as a site for positive identity work. But the opposite can also be the case. Researchers with a critical orientation may be less inclined to give interviewees the space to produce a self-esteem boosting version of what and who they are and what they do. But also without such specific intent the interview situation may include potentially problematic elements. Schwalbe and Wolkomir (2003) assume that male interviewees are eager to conform to certain cultural ideals for self-presentation and may thus be threatened by the intensive and flexible interview. They talk about a 'baseline threat' to masculinity and argue that 'to agree to sit for an interview, no matter how friendly and conversational, is to give up some control and to risk having one's public persona stripped away' (p. 58). The interview situation is 'both an opportunity for signifying masculinity and a peculiar type of encounter in which masculinity is threatened' (p. 57). If we accept this somewhat stereo-typical assumption, the interview could then be seen as a site for identity threat, as much as for providing space for positive identity work. The threatening elements would of course also trigger identity work aiming less at expressing and more at defending or repairing the identity from any possible stripping down involved in the situation. This may be problematic for the interviewer, at least the conventional one wanting to move outside interview specific constructions and access what the interviewee really does or how s/he experiences the world 'out there' – the identity project possibly central in the interview setting may interfere with and 'distort' the value and relevance of the 'truth-reporting' accounts. Presenting an 'optimal' self may be at odds with reporting 'authentic' experiences. This view seems to imply that researchers should not give too much initiative to the control-seeking, masculinity-oriented subject. In order to counter the latter there is the risk that the interview is turned into a potential battle for control. This is of course not an issue if the interviewer is satisfied with accepting the interviewee who is boosting more or less subtle forms of masculinity and counteracting identity threats, but often the research interest is to go beyond control-seeking interviewee tactics aiming at the protection of a vulnerable self.

Returning to the interview example presented above, it is easy to see how the consultant expresses a particular conception of himself – as a person taking care of those below, contributing to their development, but 'extremely sensitive' to 'wrong persons' on senior levels. Here we find a person being a caretaker and with a strong feeling for people's qualities or the lack thereof. Whether this self-understanding matches others' perception of the person or whether it is salient in many situations where the interviewee relates to hierarchy is hard to make out. The account may be said to construct an identity, not necessarily reveal one.

4 Complying and juggling with rules and resources for account production: the interview as cultural script application

In an interview situation, typically an encounter between two strangers, where one is supposed to tell the other about 'how it really is' or about one's 'true experiences' in 60 to 120 minutes, these people face a difficult task. In order not to make overwhelming demands on creativity and language skills and in order to say something that the interviewer can grasp relatively easily, accounts must rely on established cultural resources for describing the issues at hand. This means that available vocabularies, metaphors, genres and conventions for talking about issues – cultural scripts – are used. There are examples and more or less ready-made standards for how we can talk about most things – from ecological concerns to equal opportunities to our love for our children. There is, of course, more than one standard to choose between on any topic, leading to possibilities for producing culturally scripted talk in ways that do not appear inauthentic.

Cultural scripts exist on a variety of levels. Some may be shared broadly across society or in specific segments within it, e.g. an industry, occupation or class. But there may also be more local scripts, within a community or an organization. Corporate culture may be seen as a set of guidelines for, and more or less as prefabricated stories, for how one should talk about the organization. Corporate culture then offers guidelines for how organizational employees can express themselves on all sorts of issues. An illustration of this can be found in an interview within a case study of a computer consultancy firm (Alvesson, 1995). To an open question regarding whether the company was different from other companies the interviewee had worked for, the response was the relative lack of hierarchy, a flat structure: 'My only boss is X (the subsidiary manager)'. The statement reflected the script of the corporate culture, often communicated by senior managers, representing the company as non-hierarchical, with only two layers: consultants and subsidiary managers. The script-like character of the statement became clear when some minutes later in the interview the interviewee referred to another person as a superior, 'working directly under X' (and above the interviewee).

Generally, the script is typically, if not by definition, a far from nuanced and fully credible way of describing the phenomenon addressed.

Researchers will sometimes pride themselves by being able to go beyond superficiality and party line statements, but scripts are not just offered by corporate management also they are offered by other institutions and groups – professions, worker collectives – and to isolate a script following on from 'genuine' experiences and viewpoints is not an easy task. It is seldom explicitly addressed in research publications and it is even more seldom demonstrated how the researcher has dealt with this issue. Newton (1996), in locating the interview talk of an executive about the ability of a management consultancy firm to enrol him, is to some extent an exception.

Of course, the use of cultural scripts and responsiveness to moral guidelines for how one expresses oneself in interviews does not necessarily make interviews 'untrue'. Cultural scripts are not only a nuisance for the researcher. They also reduce variation and complexity and facilitate the transmitting of a package of information that is sometimes viewed as the core of an interview. In this way they make it easier for a researcher to 'collect data'. But the significance of cultural scripts creates some problems for the romantic as well as the neo-positivist, eager to get it all completely right. The point is that these standards for talking say more about 'members' methods for putting together 'a world that is recognizably familiar, orderly and moral' (Baker, 1997: 143) and less on how they experience the world in everyday life. The ambiguities and difficulties inherent in packing these experiences into 'truthful' accounts during interviews – and of course the impossibilities of doing so in responding to questionnaires – may well lead to cultural scripts taking centre stage, marginalizing the experiences and observations of a messy, contradictory world.

The common tactic of trying to move beyond scripts and other 'superficial' accounts and asking for specific examples that come closer to 'reality' may, as indicated above, be less reliable than is often imagined. Scripts may inform which examples (out of an endless number of which many can be mobilized for talks going in different directions) are picked and how these are to be framed and specifically addressed in descriptions. It may be difficult to sort out a superficial script following elements in interview talk from ingredients in the talk that really say something besides or 'outside' of (in addition to) the applying of scripts. The situation is complicated by many people's skills in using social scripts, but also in applying them in nuanced and personal ways so that they give an impression of being authentic. One overall norm complicating the use of culturally available scripts is to try to make accounts individual, original and authentic so interviewees may be inclined to try to hide the use of these scripts.

In the interview example about hierarchy talk at the beginning of the chapter, it is fairly easy to identify the presence of two scripts. One is organization-based and is emphasizing that hierarchy and meritocracy go hand in hand, that hierarchical positions are reflecting and facilitating people's development, and that a senior position means a high level of competence and a capacity to develop juniors. The other is more broadly shared in Swedish society and the fashion-oriented part of business, and says that one should have a negative attitude to or at least express reservations about hierarchy. The interview can be seen as a mix of these two scripts.

5 Moral storytelling and promotional activity: the interview as impression management

It is generally assumed that people will want to give a good impression of themselves and also of the institutions with which they identify and/ or feel they represent. We live in an economy and culture where more and more people are engaged in selling themselves and their groups or institutions. The construction of market demand is the crucial sector for increasingly large sectors where there is an overproduction – of products, services and people with educational degrees. Learning to routinely persuade others about one's virtues and offerings becomes vital in a society where advertising, branding and the use of slogans, certificates and diplomas of increasingly uncertain value and substance are quickly expanding (Alvesson, 2006). A mentality oriented towards persuasion and self-promotion is presumably also the case in a research interview setting. There are typically three broad set of ideals and virtues at stake here: rationality (efficiency, being governed by reason), social skills and morality. There will often be a positive bias in interviews in how respondents present themselves and, at least in the case of senior organizational members and professionals, the institutions they belong to and represent. Being a member of an organization, an occupation or an ethnic group often means not just the internalization of, or identification with, certain values and ideals constraining one's consciousness, but also a moral imperative to express oneself in loyal terms. This does not preclude a critique, but may still mean some (possibly non-conscious) holding back of it and an inclination to not break certain taboos.

The countermeasure to 'moral storytelling' in interviews, from the point of view of romanticism, is to establish a rapport and trust, leading to 'depth' in the contact with the subject honestly telling the truth as he or she knows it. But this is quite complicated. 'Honesty' is a moral virtue that has to be demonstrated in a particular way, e.g. through selectively revealing minor faults and errors. To appear 'honest' – and not just socially incompetent or odd – calls for impression management. As Silverman (1993: 96) says, 'maybe we feel people are at their most authentic when they are, in effect, reproducing a cultural script'. Being more personal and intimate in a social interaction does not necessary change this and what can be accomplished during a 60–90 minute interview between strangers in terms of making people willing to side-step their inclinations to do promotional work should not be exaggerated.

In studies of managers it is striking how happy they are to emphasize their moral virtues, in particular in relationship to subordinates. They often claim to be honest, considerate and free from prestige. While our interviewees come out as a bit of moral peak performers other managers they refer to are far from always at the some moral level: they can interfere too much, pretend to know more than they actually do, etc. (Alvesson, 2011).

Script-following and moral storytelling will sometimes overlap. They are not, however, the same thing. One may follow scripts in order to be able to say something easily understandable, without necessarily wanting to communicate certain positive attributes. One may, in moral storytelling, say something positive about one's self and one's affiliation in an innovative way that breaks with established conventions and scripts. The interview as impression management (moral storytelling) then points at aspects other than those focused on by the script-following metaphor. There is also sometimes an overlap between moral storytelling and identity work, but it is not the same: impression management can be done with universal means for appearing good, while identity work is about something distinct for one self and one's social group. In impression management one wants to accomplish an effect on others, while the target of identity work is one's own self.

The moral dimension comes through rather clearly in the interview example with the consultant. He is aware of the potential negative impression that his positive talk about career and hierarchy may trigger when he puts in the neutralizing statement that hierarchy 'has a tendency to sound negative', indicating that this is perhaps a misleading effect while it really, at least for him and his organization, is about care-taking and fostering, which are generally perceived as morally good. The qualities of the interviewee are also made credible through his remark about his 'extreme sensitivity' to the wrong people occupying superior positions. The interviewee then does not just adapt to hierarchy without reservations, but also puts high demands on senior people. Hierarchy and a sensitive orientation to its operations thus become constructed in such a way as to marginalize potentially negative connotations (old-fashioned, control-focused, alienating) for the benefit of qualities like overview, support and positive career development. A story of 'moralizing' hierarchy and its advocates is then one possible interpretation of the interview account.

6 Talk in the context of interests and power: the interview as political action

The romantic view on interviewing is grounded in an image of a potentially honest, unselfish subject, eager or at least willing to share his or her experiences and knowledge for the benefit of the interviewer and the research project. The interviewee then supposedly acts in the interests of science or, and more realistically, in the service of the researcher doing the interview. The interview as a moral storytelling metaphor throws some doubts on this, but one may go further and view the interview in a more explicit political perspective. The interviewee is then assumed to act in the interests of him or herself and/or the social group with which the interviewee identifies. Interviewees are then not seen just as eager to save or improve their egos or their organization's or social group's reputation and legitimacy through more or less routinized and unreflective self-promoting (or profession- or organization-promoting) statements, but as *politically aware and politically motivated actors*.

Arguably, few, if any, reports on socially significant issues are completely neutral in light of various interests. As many researchers have argued, formal institutions such as schools, municipalities and professions are political arenas and sites for struggles on how specific parts of social reality should be defined (Deetz, 1992; Pfeffer, 1981). Actors may also use interviews for their own political purposes. This does not necessarily mean that they will cheat or lie. Honesty and political awareness do not necessarily conflict. They may very well tell the (partial) truth as they know it, but in – for them – favourable ways and choose not to disclose truths anticipated to be negative towards them and the groups they feel loyal to. It would be naïve, however, to believe that manipulations, half-truths and lying are not part of what researchers may run into in fieldwork. It may also exaggerate the possibilities of a researcher as a morally uplifting force to assume that establishing a rapport and trust during an hour or so of interviewing is an efficient vehicle against opportunism and political tactics providing distortions of interview statements as reliable data. This overall theme is illustrated by a top lawyer in a big company who was interviewed by Jackall (1988), who, while during a discussion of an issue, said:

> Now, I'm going to be completely honest with you about this. (He paused for a moment and then said.) By the way, in the corporate world, whenever anybody says to you: 'I'm going to be completely honest with you about this,' you should immediately know that a curveball is on the way. But, of course, that doesn't apply to what I'm about to tell you. (p.161)

One may find it difficult to assess his subsequent telling. It may be tempting to take the first statements seriously and then assume that a curveball is indeed coming. Or to assume that as the interviewee demonstrates such an awareness and honesty about the political nature of the corporate world and is helping the researcher to understand some of its workings surely he is to be trusted. Perhaps the only thing we can learn is that these are data indicating that honesty is not a quality always expressed by people in the corporate world – and there is nothing in the interview that contradicts this, as irrespective of whether the person was lying or telling the truth (as he sees it) curveballs do sometimes arrive in corporations.

Part of the politics of interview talk comes from interviewees never being entirely sure of how a researcher will use the material gathered. Parker (2000) observed how he was perceived to be a channel of communication between the top and the bottom, feeding back information to senior management. Some managers in one company praised the General Manager in most effusive terms, probably reflecting their interest in using the research to promote themselves.

Political awareness may lead to either active constructions in accordance with one's interest or defensive moves motivated by the fear that certain 'truths' may harm oneself or the organization or occupation, which one identifies with. Such defensive moves may characterize senior people who are expected to take issues of legitimacy seriously

RETHINKING INTERVIEWS

but also characterize people at the bottom who may risk sanctions if they deviate from 'the party line'.

It is frequently difficult to sort out 'authentic experiences' from constructions that may serve the interests of a person or group. Consider the following interviewee statement by a female lawyer:

> Being a woman I think has opened to me a wider arsenal of personalities and a wider array of behaviours. Men to me tend to act the same all the time. (interviewee, cited in Ely, 1995: 623)

Whether this account reflects an 'objective reality', a genuine experience and/or the stereotypic beliefs of the interviewee or her interest in promoting her own sex as superior within the profession is hard to say (and simply gaining more data of the same sort does not necessarily make it easier).[3] It is clear, however, that the interviewee presents a statement of her own group, out of an endless number of possible ones, that is in no way neutral to various interests. It favours the flexible and broad-minded woman over the rigid and narrow-minded man on the labour market and as a candidate for promotion.[4]

A researcher may think that guarantees of anonymity – both for individual interviewees and the organization concerned – may reduce the politics of interviewing. But those interviewed may not perceive the situation in this way. They can never be certain what will happen to the material. A good tactic here for politicians, senior professionals, managers and other people in elite positions is to be very careful in how one talks, what one reveals and how one presents oneself (Jackall, 1988). As Jackall shows, a managerial career calls for being perceived as reliable and rests upon the acquired ability to smoothly manoeuvre in a tactful way, avoiding unnecessary risk-taking. A habitual act so that one cannot be tied to expressing dangerous opinions or indiscretions becomes part of the makeup of successful people in public sector and business life. It seems unlikely that interviewing, whatever the tricks are that are being used, manages to fully break with this habit. And even if interviewees could see that there are no immediate personal gains or risks calling for selfish or protective political manoeuvring in the interview situation, most of them would probably still consider the macro aspects of what they were saying. The unemployed or recipients of social welfare may not feel that as persons they face any direct threats from a specific research project, but considerations of the potential long-term policy implications of talk about underlying contingencies and the life situations of the unemployed or welfare recipients may guide which subjects will talk about these issues and the way they do so. When people in immigrant groups talk about their situation, it is also possible that they will fine tune their accounts so that they avoid reinforcing sceptical views and communicate what may be read as more positive images of themselves and their community, as was illustrated by the studies by Essers and Benschop (2007) and Fangen (2007) referred to above.

Our opening example with the senior consultant expressing views about the organizational hierarchy is presumably not an obvious illustration of politically motivated interview talk. Nevertheless, the avoidance of any negative potential features of hierarchy (limited autonomy and influence, low self-esteem, impoverished social relations, etc.) and the generally flattering view given of the corporate version of hierarchy may be seen as an expression of an awareness of constructing corporate reality in a way that is favourable for both the interviewee and the firm. Given the mainly negative view of hierarchy in large parts of contemporary Western society and the firm's reputation for emphasizing hierarchy, interview talk mainly promoting a more positive view of the latter can be seen in political terms.

7 Using language for crafting accounts: the interview as an arena for construction work

Another basic problem – given conventional ideas on the ontological status of interview accounts – concerns the nature of language and language use. There are two issues here. One is the limited possibility of language to mirror reality outside language use. Silverman (1993: 114), for example, claims that 'only by following misleading correspondence theories of truth could it have ever occurred to researchers to treat interview statements as *only* potentially accurate or distorted reports of reality'. The other issue is that people will typically use language not to optimize descriptive precision, but for productive, forward-oriented purposes, i.e. to create effects, like convincing or appearing interesting. Like people in general, persons in an interview context are not just 'truth tellers' or 'informants', but also 'use their language to do things, to order and request, persuade and accuse' (Potter and Wetherell, 1987: 32). This point is not restricted to – but can of course sometimes not entirely be separated from – issues of impression management and political interest, but relates more to the active, functional, metaphorical, contextual character of language than any particular use or misuse of language. Language use means the construction of the world, i.e. a specific version of it. Even if few people would doubt that there are 'objective' things going on 'out there' or in the minds of people, any account of these means the construction of a particular version of how things hang together and how they can be represented (Potter, 1996). 'Objective reality' is not just mirroring itself in a certain, correct language.

Even if a brilliant interviewer should manage to maximize the honesty and clarity of an interviewee's performance there are always a million aspects, words and empirical illustrations to choose between when accounting for non-trivial issues. As Hollway (1989) points out, any question can lead to an almost infinite number of answers. We have here the problem of representation, to some extent highlighted by the cultural script metaphor. Coincidence and arbitrariness always comprise unavoidable problems of representation. Whatever happens 'out there' or in terms of authentic experiences there is no self-evident correlation between this and the composition of a specific set of words. (Or as one may say, reality does not arrive with a subtext and if so, one wonders how one would have invented the latter.) The use of cultural scripts is an option but often these are not fully relevant and both interviewer and interviewee may feel that this breaks with the norm of being authentic and credible. Creativity and construction work are called for in order to produce accounts that can adapt or vary cultural scripts and/or use these as elements in more innovative interviewee work. Occasionally interviewees may move around cultural scripts in order to say something extraordinarily interesting (a really good story), but whether this is truthful or driven by a wish to say something interesting, perhaps through constructing one's experience or social practices in a dramatized way, may be hard if not impossible to ascertain.

Crafting an account is similar to authorship. Even if an interviewee tries to be precise and honest, the elements of invention and fiction are significant. People's verbal skills will differ. An account will often frequently bear the mark of people's struggle to produce that account. As Holstein and Gubrium (2003a) have observed it is not uncommon to hear respondents remark that they are not sure how to address a theme, failing to make sense of providing coherent accounts or even asking the interviewer for assistance to come up with sufficient answers. Other people address the verbal situation in an elegant way.

A good author/interviewee easily appears as credible, the verbal capacity leads to the creation of good rhetorical effects. This is grateful for the interviewer (in particular when the s/he needs to transcribe the interview and later is eager to find good citations to fill the report with.) But well articulated people capable of giving a good impression are not necessarily the same as those eager to carefully try to express impressions and experiences in a precise and nuanced way. A coherent set of interview accounts do not necessarily say more than the person is skilful in interview talk.

The locally constructed nature of interview statements thus stands in an uneasy relationship to their use in the context of a data and analysis research machinery.

Returning once more to the interview excerpt, a construction work metaphor would inspire an interpretation of the account as a creative production. Having picked 'career' as a key motivator the interviewee moves on to promotion. Promotion is then related to hierarchy – a contestable theme that calls for careful treatment. Having referred to the bad reputation of hierarchy, the interviewee then navigates away from this. One ingredient here is to become personal, thereby counteracting the somewhat impersonal, possibly alienating meaning ascribed to hierarchy. The interview starts with people in general ('most people here', 'for them'), but now expresses his own stance ('for me'). Then the virtues of hierarchy are presented. The interviewee may then anticipate the risk of being read as expressing an almost extreme pro-hierarchy position. The final statement in the excerpt, about his 'extreme sensitivity' for 'wrong persons', compensates for this. The entire account can thus be seen as an example of crafting a comprehensible and credible piece of text in light of using slippery language with multiple and sometimes negative connotations. This moving back and forth between expressing a distinct view and then softening or balancing it is then part of an exercise calling for some smoothness and an adaptation to the expectations and reactions of the (imagined) audience. The interviewee's construction work has its ingredients of dramatization, indicating the desire to say something interesting, e.g. 'most people here are heavily focused on their career' and, in particular, 'then I am extremely sensitive to when there are wrong individuals on top. How in hell could they get there ...?'. This may of course reflect a true subjectivity, but may also be an expression of the anticipated task of crafting an interesting account.

8 Language as constituting the interviewee: the interview as a play of the powers of discourse

Poststructuralists would challenge the idea of the conscious, autonomous, holistic and clearly defined individual as the bearer of meaning and as an active and 'acting' subject around which the social world rotates (e.g. Deetz, 1992; Foucault, 1980; Hollway, 1984; Weedon, 1987). Assumptions about the individual as a coherent, unique and, in terms of motivation and cognition, more or less integrated universe – a dynamic centre for consciousness, emotions, evaluations and actions – are viewed as problematic (Geertz, 1983: 59). Of course, this critique strikes at the heart of neo-positivists' and romantics' conception of the interview subject, assuming that the interviewee has 'knowledge', although in a non-articulated and unrefined form, and is a subject who is willing and capable of communicating this.

The poststructuralists would want to shift the focus from the autonomous individual to a linguistic and discursive context, which socially creates forms and expressions of subjectivity limited in time and space.[5] Language is not an expression of subjectivity; rather – it is claimed – it is what *constitutes* subjectivity. From this it follows that subjectivity is frequently unstable, ambiguous – a discourse-driven process rather than a structure. Thinking and actions 'depend on the circulation between subjectivities and discourses which are available' (Hollway, 1984: 252). The presence of a powerful discourse may stabilize subjectivity, but the plurality of discourse in people's lives typically encourages varied and fluctuating subjectivities.

Discourses are not produced or mastered by the individual, they rather speak of him or her in that available discourses position that person in the world in a particular way prior to them having any sense of choice. Discourses (as the concept is used by Foucault and his followers), refer to a system of thought carried by a specific language and anchored in social practices. It frames and forms individuals. In terms of interviewing, this understanding would see the situation as an outcome of the discourses being present, constituting the subject and her talk. The accounts produced are mainly of interest as indications of the discourses at play and powers over the individual subject (Foucault, 1980). Prior (1997: 70) has argued that 'a representation should be understood, not as a true and accurate reflection of some aspect of an external world, but as something to be explained and accounted for through the discursive rules and themes that predominate in a particular socio-historical context'. Some of the relevant rules and themes can then be understood as related to the 'interview society', e.g. the idea that the normal individual is to be turned into a subject who is willing and capable of expressing their inner self in brief and pre-planned talks with strangers. Any sign of unwillingness or an incapacity to account for one's self or experiences or to report about the world one has observed is viewed as being indicative of a lack of openness or trust in other people and thus possibly a source of personal inadequacy, doubt and shame.

This metaphor to some extent parallels the one of the interview as identity works (metaphor 3 above). The identity concept, however, privileges cognitions and feelings associated with the self-concept, while the interview as a play of discourse metaphor, as used here, puts an emphasis on a particular form of language use associated with discourses and its capacity to sweep subjectivity along with it. Rather than the individual struggling to construct an identity through accounts, the metaphor discussed in this section suggests that discourse constitutes the individual. The discourse power metaphor also shows some similarity with the issue treated in the previous section (interview as construction work). Both problematize the relationship between discourse and subject. It is not the knowing subject but language that takes the upper hand. But while the construction work metaphor emphasizes how the individual tries to use language but is caught by its slippery and ambiguous nature, the power of discourse view focuses on how language is operating on, and thus producing, a version of the interviewee subject. The discourse power play metaphor does *not*, however, focus on how the subject is constructing reality in light of the problem of representation, but on how the discourses are making themselves present in the interview situation, working on the subject and giving primacy to how s/he 'carries' certain constitutions of the social world. The interviewee is then seen (almost) as a puppet on the string of the discourse(s).[6]

Returning to the illustrative case of the senior consultant addressing hierarchy, a Foucauldian-inspired reading may note how a particular career discourse, assuming that people can be ranked and ordered in a hierarchical manner and that, at least for some, subordinating themselves to a corporate machinery, speaks through the interviewee. The statement is then read as reflecting the power of this discourse, perhaps constituting the interviewee subject rather than any facts about the organization or the authentic beliefs and values of the interviewee.

Summarizing the framework

The overall framework is portrayed in Figure 5.1. Here the aspects indicated by the eight metaphors plus the two 'conventional' views on

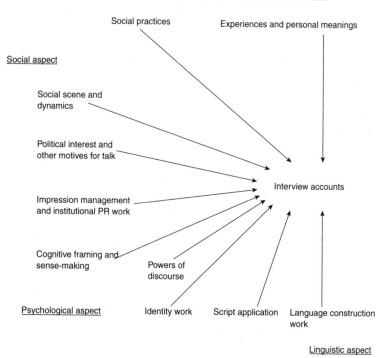

Figure 5.1 A framework for reflexive thinking about research interviews

interviews are included. Together they indicate the spectrum of what can be seen as the major 'sources' of (logics, mechanisms behind) interview statements. I have added some key dimensions (reality out there, social mechanisms, psychology and language issues) that to various degrees are central for what informs what interviewees say. The arrows in Figure 5.1 indicate forces possibly influencing or likely to influence the interview talk. We can seldom know what combinations of potential influencing ingredients matter most in individual cases. It is important to bear all this in mind and to make efforts to sort out which are most significant, adapting our understandings, ambitions and techniques accordingly. More about this in later chapters.

Working through the metaphors: example two

The metaphors all suggest a move in focus from the researcher controlling the interview as an instrument to the situation and to some extent the interviewee, whose talk is affected by many other circumstances than the researcher's interventions and the capacity and willingness of the interviewee to report about the social world or express his/her genuine experiences.

All eight metaphors can, in principle, be used on any empirical material, although they may be more or less relevant or useful in specific cases. I illustrated this with references to the interview with a management consultant, described at the beginning of the chapter. To follow this up, a very brief additional example will do. This one is picked from the literature and comes from a study of a large industrial company in the UK. The interview is with a senior manager, a former engineer, who refers to projects that have been cancelled because 'they tried to do too much', were too expensive and too late, and blames the 'British engineering culture'. This person describes the corporate situation as follows:

> We've got to move from an engineering-led culture to a market-led one. If railway engineers think they can run the trains because they like running trains, rather than running them for passengers, they then will end up out of a job. (Senior manager, interviewed in Watson, 1994: 152)

This kind of statement is not uncommon in interviews. It may be seen as expressing a 'truth' about corporate affairs or the true beliefs and values of the interviewee. It may also be read as being related to the specific scene – in an interview with a professor from a business school this appears to be an appropriate statement (the first of my eight metaphors above). The interviewee may assume that this is the kind of thing that fits with the research project (2). In the talk the person – a former engineer – constructs himself as market-oriented (3). He follows scripts for talking – production-orientation is outdated while market-oriented is what one should be (4). The statement also gives a favourable impression through adopting the morally superior position of doing things for customers rather than for one's own egocentric taste (5). The interviewee thereby adopts a position that is assumed to be legitimate and politically correct (6). In terms of trying to represent what is perceived to be going on, or what should be going on, a messy, ambiguous corporate reality is neatly ordered through either being an 'engineering-led culture' or a 'market-led' one perhaps neglecting that technically good performances are probably crucial for customers (7). The contemporary dominating discourse on market-orientation speaks through the interviewee, perhaps best seen as a passive site for this discourse (8). It would have been interesting to observe whether he would have produced the same kind of account if interviewed by a person from an engineering school instead. Perhaps this had hampered the strong and clear message of needing to move from an engineering-led to a market-led culture. But if the same or a similar statement had also been made to an interviewer with an engineering background, it would have weakened the relevance of some of the interpretations from the metaphors presented in this book and reinforced a more conventional reading of the interview as being about corporate affairs or the interviewee's personal views on these.

Conclusion

The eight metaphors suggested here summarize a great deal of the theoretical knowledge that is of relevance for an intellectual – as opposed to a technical or means-optimizing – view of the interview. Some of these metaphors are in various ways addressed in the methodology literature, others are perhaps novel or at least less commonly discussed. No doubt many qualitative researchers have systematically or intuitively thought about at least some of the issues addressed. But even if many researchers occasionally downplay or even disregard obviously superficial or self-promoting interviews, I would argue that in the majority of cases the researcher should take interview statements very seriously and treat them as 'data' providing the cornerstone of empirical inquiry. There must be clear indications of the interviews not working as producers of useful data before they are met with scepticism and/or rejected. Taking the eight metaphors seriously would suggest a reverse interpretive logic: one must have very good reasons to believe that interview statements indicate reality (objective or subjective) before paying any particular attention to them as valuable indicators of anything other than interview talk and the logics or forces producing this. That they may appear trustworthy or seem to point to some examples illustrating general claims or ideas does not necessarily say that much.

Using the eight metaphors is not intended to offer a complete framework in which all components need to be accepted and used. The idea is to inspire more sophisticated thinking and this can be done in different ways. Perhaps a more limited set of metaphors or the use of others (or other types of synthesis) may be helpful for the individual researcher (I discussed this in Chapter 4). The experience of the interviewer and the nature of the research topic matter here. Interview research on (mainly) individual and emotionally sensitive matters such as a fear of dying, a relation to children, experiences of chronic illness or of having lived with a violent partner, may differ from studies aiming at more social issues (such as an assessment of foreign politics, responses to the professionalization of one's occupation or views on environmental crises). Rather than embrace the eight metaphors as a universal pre-scription for how to think about interviews, in addition to or as an alternative to considering them as instruments or knowledge-producing human encounters, many researchers may benefit from finding a line of thinking and some powerful reference points that work specifically for them. This may be more general or in a specific project. But I do think that aggregated insights from social science as a whole suggest that we think through these eight central aspects and potentially take at least some of these seriously.

As with metaphors in general, when employed to think through how we imagine and give meaning to various phenomena, the ones here suggested may be useful for a) mapping available positions to the subject matter (research interview); b) encouraging more informed choices about how we can relate to it; and c) supporting more creative research practices. The idea of a metaphor is less to give an exact map than to encourage productive lines of thinking.

I will in the next chapter develop some ideas along these lines on how the framework, or a version of it or similar (multiple-reference points), can be employed. Here, critical imagination and reflexivity will often need to reconcile with pragmatic concerns.

Notes

1 This metaphor basically summarizes the localist view on the interview.
2 Female researchers especially will frequently use private settings in order to establish better contact (e.g. Martin, 1992; Skeggs, 1994).
3 An interesting question here is how we could assess a male interviewee producing the same statement, i.e. saying that as a man I act the same all the time, while women are much more flexible and varied. This is possibly also a stereotypical opinion. There is, however, no self-evident political interest in degrading one's own category. However, sometimes people may want to give an impression of being reflective and progres-sive in gender issues, which can benefit them. However, this form of mixed positioning in terms of distancing oneself from one's own (bad)

social category would typically be less significant than for a person self-promoting the category s/he is a part of.

4   Many feminists and other writers on gender will also to some extent emphasize the superiority of women in terms of a more flexible or less prestigious or control-oriented leadership or working style (e.g. Eagly & Carli, 2007), even though more nuanced researchers think that this is only a very modest difference. Irrespective of the advantages and problems with this approach (see Alvesson & Billing, 2009, for a critical discussion) it may supply people with scripts for how to talk about gender at work.

5   Subjectivity refers to the individual's conscious and unconscious thoughts, emotions and perceptions, the individual's self-insight and attitude to the surrounding world.

6   This metaphor may be criticized for ascribing too much strength to discourse and assuming a too weak subject (Alvesson & Kärreman, 2000b; Newton, 1998). As a potentially inspiring countermetaphor to dominant conceptions, it may, however, like the others proposed here, be productive. One could add that Foucauldians soften the view of the discourse-driven individual through the idea that power is always imperfect and that there is always resistance often leading to discourse temporarily weakening or losing its grip – a point made also by Scheurich (1997) and referred to above.

6

REFLEXIVITY: A FRAMEWORK

Readers interested in social facts or meanings may now feel some unease and might even ask what is the point in doing interviews at all. Perhaps the status of interview talk is so uncertain and the interpretations so difficult that it is wise to avoid doing or at least seriously relying on interviews in research. It is *not*, however, my intention to make an extremely strong case against the instrumental use of interviews. Considering the set of the metaphors proposed in the previous chapter is not necessarily incoherent with the ambition of, when motivated, using interview statements to obtain knowledge about the social world or people's experiences. While localists and others (poststructuralists, advocates of observational methods) have delivered important critiques of neo-positivist as well as romantic notions of interviewing, it would be premature to ban this method or to use it exclusively in 'minimalistic' ways, e.g. studying interview talk solely as a local accomplishment and treating accounts as the object of study. We can learn much more from interviewees than how they talk about various subject matters in specific social situations. As with all critiques, it may be too harsh and taken too far, sacrificing relevance for rigor. But more of the latter is often called for and interview researchers (and also many others relying on their data) need to think through what they are doing and be more self-critical about the assumptions, work, results and claims.

Reflexive pragmatism

A possible response to the complexity and richness of qualitative interviews indicated by the eight metaphors is by means of a careful interpretation of the extent to which accounts may be used for a variety of research purposes and how this may be done. What is proposed here is a reflexive pragmatist approach to the research interview. The increasingly popular concept reflexivity is used in a variety of ways (Alvesson et al., 2008; Brewer, 2000: 126–133; Lynch, 2000). The perhaps most common one emphasizes that the researcher is part of the social world that is studied and this calls for exploration and self-examination.

The notion of reflexivity sometimes leads to a preoccupation with the researcher-self and its significance for the research process. Individual backgrounds and other personal issues of relevance for inter-actions with those studies are then highlighted (e.g. Hollway & Jefferson, 2000). This can also lead to forms of writing placing a researcher's personal experience during the research process at the centre (confes-sional tales; Van Maanen, 1988) or may trigger intensive explorations of the various researcher-selves that are active in the process (Reinharz, 1997). Hertz (1997: viii) suggests for example that interviewers need to 'have an on-going conversation about experience while simultanously living in the moment'. At worst, this may lead to researchers being inclined 'to give a cleansing account of their positions, preconceptions and interests' (Lee & Hassard, 1999: 396).

I am using reflexivity here in a somewhat different sense, focusing more on the interview situation, the interviewee and the accounts produced rather than on the interviewer, although this book probably also offers fuel for a 'researcher/self-focused' type of reflexivity. Even though the outcome of the interview, the text, is of course crucial, it is not the exclusive focus of concern. Potter (1997: 146), advocating a localist approach, emphasizes a focus on the details of the text. He suggests that 'reflexivity encourages us to consider the way a text such as this is a version, selectively working up coherence and incoherence, telling historical stories, presenting and, indeed, constituting an objec-tive, out-there reality'. For me, this text focus offers important food for consideration, but still suggests too narrow a domain.

Reflexivity for me stands for conscious and consistent efforts to view the subject matter from different angles, strongly avoiding the a priori privileging of a favoured one, including a focus on the details of texts. Rorty (1989) talks about irony implying a constant awareness that there are always other vocabularies for addressing the line taken. One approach is to move between different lines of interpretation, varying and confronting an earlier used vocabulary with a line of interpretation that offers a different angle with a different vocabulary (Alvesson & Sköldberg, 2009). This means challenging the chosen interpretation and the researcher confronting him or herself and possibly the reader with alternative views, which may facilitate arriving at the 'strongest' or most interesting interpretation and/or offering alternative ones, in which the study may offer more than one type of result. Let me give an example. The political action metaphor, for example, challenges the more conventional neo-positive 'tool' and romantic 'human encounter' metaphors, but one could also turn the situation around, arguing that although individuals will seldom act totally without political awareness and self-interests they may also perceive the situation in other terms, and may be enrolled in projects appealing to other motives such as sharing insights, helping the researcher, etc. The ideal is to maintain an awareness that there is more than one good way of understanding something and there is a great risk that the one chosen may hide or repress equally (or even more) plausible or valuable alternative interpretations. Reflexivity means working with multiple interpretations in order to steer away from traps and to produce rich and varied results. Reflexivity may be something that the researcher engages in during the analysis (before 'writing it up'), but it may more or less strongly affect text work and be explicit in the completed text. In other words, one may consider limiting reflexivity mainly to considerations behind the scene and letting the produced text be the result of the reflexive thinking, or one may incorporate parts of the process of reflexivity in the published text. The latter involves inviting the reader to see how the researcher considers various interpretations or vocabularies and confronts these, thus opening this up for the reader to consider problems, uncertainties and alternative interpretations.

Pragmatism here means a willingness to postpone some doubt and still use the material for the best possible purpose(s). Pragmatism builds on an awareness that time, space and patience are not unlimited and are a withholding of limitless reflexivity. It also means an occasional bracketing of radical doubt and self-critique for the achievement of results. There is a need here to balance reflexive ideals with the idea of 'delivering knowledge'. Results are, however, informed by reflexive considerations of how the empirical material can be interpreted. The knowledge produced may thus be quite different from what was intended at the start of a research process. Research results may also be multiple in character. One can point to several possible interpretations – preferably all of these should be empirically supported and interesting – and then

REFLEXIVITY: A FRAMEWORK

offer several potential contributions. This may mean several worthy insights or several good questions are raised. An absence of any clear and conclusive evidence that this is the best way to understand something does not mean that good results have not been produced. Often there are reasons for seeing the world in more than one way. This view on good research then is *not* the same as a general vagueness or indecisiveness in producing results.

Reflexive pragmatism calls for an epistemological awareness rather than a philosophical rigor. Jumping between paradigms is a very difficult skill, but it is not impossible to widen and vary one's horizon by looking self-critically at favoured assumptions and lines of inquiry. In order to facilitate such a reflexive pragmatist approach, we need to have a fairly broad and multi-angled theoretical understanding of the research interview (and, by implication, similar social interactions in general). The eight metaphors are instrumental here. Each represents a starting point and some broad guidelines for theoretical – as opposed to technical – reasoning about the subject matter.

R&D reflexivities[1]

Reflexive practices might usefully be differentiated between those that emphasize problematic or 'dangerous' things – intellectually, politically or ethically – and those that try to produce new insights. The former indicates problems and uncertainties with efforts to establish how things are, whether it is objective truth, authentic experiences or superior theoretical insights. I refer to this as D-reflexivity: D stands for deconstruction, defensiveness and destabilization. The latter is about challenging a discourse, an interpretation, a concept or a representation in order to produce an alternative, better or supplementary knowledge contribution. I call the latter, more 'positive' work, R-reflexivity: R refers to reconstruction, re-presentation and rethinking (Alvesson et al., 2008). There are of course no absolute distinctions between these two; the border is to some extent floating.

D-reflexivity

D-reflexivity practices challenge orthodox understandings by pointing out the limitations of, and uncertainties behind, the manufactured unity and coherence of texts, including claims based on data as well as the way in which conformism, institutional domination and academic fashion may account for the production of particular knowledge. A major resource for D-reflexivity is (a selective use of) postmodernism (Alvesson, 2002). This approach encourages researchers to see the social world as basically open, ambiguous and indecidable. It means a confrontation with dominant views on knowledge, privileging certainty, closure and authoritative research results, whether this is about social facts or meaning. As expressed by Scheurich:

> The researcher then fills this indeterminate openness with her/his interpretive baggage, imposes names, categories, constructions, conceptual schemes, theories upon the unknowable, and believes that the indeterminate is now located, constructed, known. Order has been created. The restless, appropriate spirit of the researcher is (temporarily) at peace. (1997: 74)

From this perspective, categories used by researchers and other people do not reveal the truth; they don't simply assist us in developing frameworks and describing phenomena so that knowledge providing insights about the world can be developed. 'Categories' here refer to concepts seen as capable of assisting the sorting and naming of the chunks of reality studied by researchers. Categories impose order, they structure the world according to a particular logic. Categories are not only valuable tools for understanding but also mechanisms for power and control that fixate our ways of seeing. They are not so much sources of misunderstandings as basic ingredients in forms of understanding that are often insufficiently reflected upon and problematized and also frequently used in ways that give too little space for uncertainty and variation. Skeptical approaches like Foucauldian power-knowledge analysis or critical theory ideas can be used for D-reflexivity, as can the localist approaches I reviewed in Chapter 2. However, these approaches also need to be targeted by other viewpoints and exposed to critique.

D-reflexivity engages with the problems, uncertainties and social contingencies of knowledge claims – whether these are empirical claims, concepts or theoretical propositions. By emphasizing how social science orders and freezes the world in a particular way, power/knowledge connections are illuminated and truth-creating effects are disarmed. These practices are conducted in attempts to counteract 'harm' – challenging efforts to stabilize the view of the world in a particular, problematic way, as well as to expose the unreflective reproduction of dominant vocabularies, rules or conventions in social research.

R-reflexivity

R-reflexivity is about developing and adding something; a person engaged in R-reflexivity is in the (re-)construction rather than the demolition industry. It means bringing in issues of alternative paradigms, root metaphors, perspectives, vocabularies, lines of interpretation, political values, and representations; re-balancing and re-framing voices independent of any empirical material in order to interrogate the material in a more fundamental way. Instances of alternative constructions and reconstructions of fundamental elements of the research project are central to these reflexive practices. R-reflexive practices are employed to illuminate what is left out and marginalized: the (almost) missed opportunity, premature framing, the reproduction of received wisdom, the re-enforcement of power relations and unimaginative labelling. They provide alternative descriptions, interpretations, results, vocabularies, voices and points of departure that can be taken into account and can show some of the differences they would make. R-reflexivity aims to open up new avenues, paths and lines of interpretation to produce 'better' research ethically, politically, empirically and theoretically.

Of the contemporary popular perspectives with a relevance for methodology, postmodernism/poststructuralism is of course mainly about D-reflexivity, as the aim of most of its versions is to undermine positive claims to results and contributions. Most others contribute more to R-reflexivity in that they encourage a consideration of alternative views, even though localist approaches also have a strong D-potential.[2] At the same time, this should not be exaggerated. When I talk about D- and R-reflexivity it is with a reference to alternative contributions following on from reflexive projects, where the overall interplay between and confrontation of different points of view are central. D and R moments are always involved. An interview as a tool or human encounter-based view can be used for the reinterpretation and undermining of, for example, a Foucauldian or political interpretation and can thereby create D-reflexivity effects.

Reflexive research can be seen as engaging in practices that create a dialectic between D-reflexivity and R-reflexivity. This means moving between tearing down – pointing at the weaknesses in a text and disarming truth claims – and developing something new or different, where the anxieties of offering positive knowledge do not hold researchers back. This can be applied both to interpretations of an interview statement and to broader lines of reasoning based on these (and, of course, on other materials).

Reflexive methodology in use

A reflexive approach means working with a framework involving a set of potential lines of thinking and theoretical ideas about how to understand a subject matter, rather than a definitive theoretical formulation and privileged vocabulary for grasping it. It means opening up and acknowledging the uncertainty of all empirical material and knowledge claims, but also offering alternative lines of interpretation for how to use the interview material in thoughtful and creative ways. It does not give privilege to a particular ontology (a specific view of the nature of social reality) but can in principle be combined with various paradigms and specific theories. At the same time reflexivity in action may well mean that various initially held positions and approaches are not left intact, as reflexivity means challenging and reconsidering assumptions and beliefs about what data are all about. In this sense it shares some characteristics with critical theories questioning received wisdoms and opening up a plurality of meanings (Alvesson & Deetz, 2000). Reflexivity aims to inspire a dynamic, flexible way of working with empirical material and to escape a simple theory/method divide.

The eight metaphors mentioned previously when combined with the meta-theoretical framework proposed here can not only give a fairly holistic view (or meta-view) on interviews, but can also be seen as offering *examples* of what can be included in an interpretive repertoire that would be useful in exploring how empirical interview material can be conceptualized and rich meanings be produced. Combining all or, given one's inclinations and research project, some of these with the 'tool' and 'human encounter' metaphors in a repertoire of viewpoints means that the complexity and richness of interviews are acknowledged. One is thus quite open about the possibility that there is no definite meaning or truth reflected or indicated in interviews. This calls for a preparedness to employ various 'seeing as'-approaches in addressing them. This does not mean, of course, that all such angles are equally productive and worth developing in specific instances. The set of metaphors can offer resources for knowledge-development and reflexivity, although using these in a rigid way would counteract the ideal of reflexivity.

The framework suggested here can be applied to, or combined with, any home-base positions on interviews, i.e. any basic outlook on and preference for using interviews. For example, one can start by seeing and trying to use the interview as an instrument, but then be open to the possibility that other understandings may be more insightful and that occasionally one may be motivated to not stick to this initial view. This means a more or less radical re-consideration and opening up of how one should proceed from the preferred position. The conventional neo-positivist and romantic assumptions about facts to be collected or stable meanings to be interpreted are not necessarily reproduced without friction in a research process that takes the epistemology proposed here seriously. Some of the metaphors are strongly 'non-positivist', but elements of the thinking they inspire can be incorporated in efforts to make neo-positivist research more rigorous (see next section). One may want to use structured interviews to find out how things are or work (social facts), but may then scrutinize if and when the interview accounts really say this. Some of the metaphors challenge the narrow localist view of studying language use in a micro-setting through encouraging an interest in, for example, wider discourses and organizational politics. The idea with the set of metaphors is that they should be broadly useful in inquiry, irrespective of where the researcher comes from and anticipates he or she will go. As has been said already, different metaphors and combinations of these may, however, be useful in different ways, to different degrees, for different researchers and different research projects. Flexibility is important here. A key component is of course what is actually happening in a specific interview. Any of the logics or lines of actions indicated by the eight metaphors and/ or the expression of authentic experiences or the reporting of external events may be more or less relevant in order to interpret the talk produced in an interview – and to challenge the favoured interpretations.

Working with reflexivity and metaphors as proposed in this book can be combined with various 'method positions' along the spectrum of social facts (neo-positivism), meanings (romanticism) and language use (localism), or a combination thereof. One may work with a combination of a particular position and (a variety of) metaphors, or simply downplay, even bypass the three method-positions mentioned and emphasize the metaphors in relation to how one is working with the production, interpretation and presentation of empirical material. My two empirical examples in the previous chapter (the senior consultant on hierarchy and the executive on being market-led) indicated a way of working with the interview material without necessarily a priori locating oneself as focusing on facts, meanings or language use.

In terms of developing a framework for empirical inquiry the reflexivity-metaphor thinking introduced here may perhaps be seen as in some ways as a challenge and an alternative to, in other ways a complement to other conventional ingredients in the set-up of a research project. As it slices the significant elements in research differently, and in particular transcends the conventional theory/method divide, it calls for some rethinking of what is needed. It may, for example, downplay the significance of the procedural and technical aspects of method. It may also postpone the need for a strict research question at the outset of research. The incorporation of theoretical ideas in the methodology (reflexivity, metaphors) may to some extent reduce the need for a strong theoretical framework, as conventionally defined, i.e. as separate from methodology. But there is no set formula for how to work with these ingredients.

My point is that the epistemological ideas suggested here should not be seen as another complication that simply adds an additional burden for the researcher. It is intended as a way of thinking about how we can avoid getting caught in certain ways, but also as a way of making life easier for that researcher by offering an alternative way of thinking about knowledge generation and using interview material in realistic as well as innovative ways. As (social) theory is built into the methodology, the interpretive work becomes strengthened and it becomes easier to make a theoretical contribution.

The reflexive approach can be formulated in dialectical terms: point of departure, negation, transcendence. One starting point here is the dominant view(s) on interviews: this 'theory' states that an interview is a tool or human encounter in which a knowledge-transmitting logic prevails; language is a transparent medium for the communication of insights, experiences and facts. The interviewee is motivated by a desire to assist science; is called upon in a sufficient well-structured or secure and personal way that pretence and role-play does not matter much and that true or authentic answers are provided. The interviewee is – or can be mobilized as – an integrated and competent source of meaning, knowledge and intentionality, etc. The metaphors then offer counter-views, negating this understanding in favour of a different kind of theorizing: e.g. the interviewee as a political actor rather than a truth teller; as controlled by and within discourse rather than as a language user in control of meaning, etc. The metaphors are not necessarily, however, to be read as expressing superior truths about interviews, but may be seen as theoretical inputs in stretching the imagination, openness and theoretical-methodological vocabulary so that some mistakes in using interviews are avoided and any possibilities are utilized better. This then calls *not* for a priori favouring of a (set of) metaphor(s) or counterview(s) (as in localism), but for an openness towards the spectrum of positions possible and to see what a reasonable compromise would be between the research questions asked and a methodological awareness in relation to specific empirical materials. More about this in the next section on implications.

Taking one step away from the metaphors suggested and opening up more strongly to giving conventional concerns a chance, could require us to see interview situations and accounts as highly ambiguous and a complex blend of knowledge-expressing elements with social, political, psychological and discursive processes. The processes highlighted by the eight counter-metaphors may not necessarily dominate. Instead of viewing interviews as an expression of local dynamics one may be open to the possibility of interviewees being capable of abstracting from local specificity. The scene always matters but not necessarily in a very strong way.[3] A counterpoint to the political metaphor could be to suggest that self-interest is not the sole motive for human beings and that, dependending on the questions raised and the position taken by the interviewee, s/he can also be mobilized through motives such as curiosity or an intellectual interest in research or, more generally, a better understanding of the subject matter investigated (Kreiner & Mouritsen, 2005). The metaphor 'informant' may be appropriate. But that this is the best – or even an appropriate – view of an interviewee should not be taken for granted. It needs to be demonstrated and not assumed in interview-based research.

Interview accounts needs to be read in a variety of ways. The themes that interviewers will typically try to address – reality 'out' or 'in there' – can often put some kind of imprint on accounts. But so can various other issues. The relevance of different metaphors is related to the research questions asked, careful considerations of critical reflection of what kind of ontological claims the material can carry and, in particular, the productivity and innovativeness of the interpretations made.

Interview material is then carefully interpreted considering a wide set of meanings and complications and remembering that any interpretation of interview material is founded on an analysis of the local context, political motives, the slipperiness and powers of language, etc.

that may make it difficult to use for conventional analysis. The researcher should provide strong reasons for giving interview material a certain ontological status, in particular if it is seen as referring to social phenomena out there or the interior (level of meaning) of the interviewee and his/her preferences. As indicated by many of the metaphors suggested above, to treat interview material as discourse – examples of language use in which a particular view on social reality is constructed (not revealed) – is, of course, a possibility (Alvesson & Kärreman, 2000a, b; Grant et al., 1998). The gap between the empirical material (interview talk) and what it is supposed to refer to (language use in organizations) is not that large, even though as Boje (1991) observes, the former does not capture the process and performance dimensions that are so crucial in language use in organizational situations. And discourse (talk) produced in an interview situation may differ from discourse (talk) produced in other situations, so one can't just draw conclusions on the latter that are based on the first without having good reasons for doing so.

An illustration

In this section I will present an extract from an interview and then discuss some possible interpretations in light of the understanding of interviews outlined above, thus illustrating some of my points.

The interview is with a senior consultant and project manager in a very large management consultancy company (it is actually the same firm as my first interview example came from, but with another person: see the beginning of Chapter 4). The interviewee was in his early thirties and I was interviewing him as part of a large project on the organization and work in management consultancy firms. Parts of the interview were about project work and how that company controlled it more generally, parts of it concerned a specific, recently completed consultancy project. In one rather interesting part, the interviewee – talking more generally about his work – said:

> Well, I have large degrees of freedom in what I do so that we can deliver what we should and absolutely the most important is quality and then the economy comes in second. We are very eager to avoid a bad reputation, as in this project where we had one person that the client felt a bit uncertain about whether he really had the necessary qualities, and then we put in a

> more senior person during some days providing extra support so that the client should feel more comfortable. This means an extra cost that you have to take ... but this is acceptable.

While this account may seem to indicate the significance of 'quality' one may point to the uncertainties regarding what this term is supposed to refer to. The interview account seems to indicate that quality is making the client happy and avoiding any doubt or worry on his or her behalf. On the other hand, quality may be seen as a guideline that is central and that also signs of somebody anticipating quality problems are taken very seriously, promptly triggering measures to improve the situation. Quality is then a value that 'is absolutely the most important' (as the interviewee puts it), possibly irrespective of how the client perceives it. (The relationship between 'quality as such', as an absolute value, and the client worrying or not worrying about it may be uncertain and varied. One can imagine that the client, perhaps being in a weaker position than the consultant to assess what the latter actually is doing, may worry about quality problems without any good reason for doing so, or be confident and faithful at the same time as there are unspotted quality problems and good 'objective' reasons for worrying.) The case may be read as showing a sensitivity to client worries and as 'proving' or illustrating how absolutely central 'quality' is for this organization.

Later in the interview, when budgeting and planning are addressed, the interviewee claimed that the company was fairly accurate in its estimations, although sometimes things did not work out exactly as planned.

> I think we are fairly accurate ... in a systems project then the system has to work and you can't pull any tricks anywhere, but if it is softer areas where you work with organizational development or employee education and so on, then you can 'cheat' so that you stick to the plans, in terms of how deeply or broadly you do things.

This account points at how quality matters differ with respect of the degree to which errors and suboptimal solutions will be detected. Quality is the most significant value for the company, according to the first, general account, but if it is possible to get away with certain tricks and save money then it appears to be less important than keeping to the budget, according to the second account. Arguably, doing something 'less deeply or broadly' will be at the expense of 'quality', if 'quality' is defined as doing a very good job. If quality is defined as the client being happy and not directly noticing errors or slightly suboptimal solutions ('quality as successful cheating'), then the two parts of the interview are well in line. But then quality refers to 'what you can get away with', without dissatisfying the client or oneself getting a bad reputation. However, what quality stands for in this account and in most others is very unclear and notoriously ambiguous. Despite, or rather because of this, quality is talked about and its significance underscored. This of course is not just the case for this company but for all organizations in a variety of situations. It is a kind of standard talk that people produce as self-evident in interactions such as interviews with researchers and conversations with clients. One can't really say anything else other than 'quality' is important. When this word is invoked it is almost always followed by something positive. Quality talk fulfils a legitimating role.

But when moving on to something else then the meaning of the value of quality becomes uncertain or marginalized. The second quotation indicates that quality is not always that important, after all, the key thing here is that the interviewee is not using the Q-word. In this case keeping the budget on target seems to be the first priority. The discrepancy between the accounts can be seen in terms of different economic contexts and discourses. The first account circles around client relations and 'quality': here quality is absolutely the most important ingredient. The second deals with management control and financial results: here quality is less important in relation to keeping the budget. The discourse invoked here then produces another version of the corporate world and its priorities than the client orientation discourse: according to the latter, 'quality' is 'absolutely the most important', while the former says that keeping to budget ranks higher.

This case illustrates the problem of viewing interviewees as integrated and stable sources of knowledge. The discourses being invoked in the situation in a sense take over and produce certain kinds of statements. This case also illustrates the difficulties in nailing down social reality. Quality talk and various more or less symbolic acts in order to communicate seriousness in the commitment to 'quality' may be registered, but there may not be any stable and integrated ideas and meanings held by subjects or specific objective quality characteristics that we can determine. Expressing a concern for quality may be seen as a political act. Variation in the accounts in the interview may reflect the social interaction: the different themes of talk during different parts of the interview create different local contexts of talk, produce different rankings of guiding values. Making insertions about something outside the interview situation based on the interview material is thus difficult. This is not a matter of it here being just a single interview (an excerpt from one). Other interviews will not necessarily lead to clarity. Listening to a number of people perhaps saying something similar (or very diverse) does not mean that one can come any closer to obtaining robust knowledge about the orientations of people or the objective practices of the company. Confronting an interviewee with possible contradictions may be a possibility (though not used in the interview cited here), but may easily lead to efforts to create an impression of coherence or other defensive operations. Whether efforts to clarify and specify 'quality' can lead to clarity and coherence or new incoherencies is uncertain. Sometimes coherence is created because the interviewee is motivated to avoid and capable of avoiding varied talk more than follow-up questions leading to zooming in on the truth beyond incoherent and confusing talk. Such coherence may be reassuring for the interviewer, but may give a misleading impression of having robust knowledge. This may lead to attention being diverted away from illuminating the possible varied and not easily aligned ways in which people relate to and are guided by ideals such as 'quality' and reaching the budget. It may here be better to allow an interviewee to talk freely about these issues and not to expect and encourage coherence through asking questions that will trigger moves in this direction. (When several interviews are conducted, of course, one tactic may be to be confrontational in a couple of these, something perhaps best done in the final part of the interviews. I'll come back to this in the next chapter.)

The example illustrates some of the problems of taking interview material as given and the need to consider it in relationship to the local social context as well as to the more or less conscious political orientations of people interested in portraying themselves and their organizations in moral and rational terms. (However, a moral orientation does not come fully via the less morally sensitive area of keeping to the budget. Here modest 'cheating' seems to be acceptable as a sign of rationality.) Doing interviews so that a topic is framed in different ways may be helpful – talking about clients and budget control means that 'quality' appears differently – in order to check for incoherence and a fluidity of meaning. Interpreting the interview accounts more carefully through considering aspects encouraged by poststructuralism and localism may lead to an appreciation of the shaky nature of accounts as 'mirroring' meanings or facts. New and perhaps more interesting research questions, such as the tactics and contingencies of quality claims, may be triggered and replace more conventional questions.

All the same, it seems possible as well to use the interview to move somewhat beyond looking only at the context-specific constructions of the consultancy work in relationship to clients, client satisfaction, quality and budget considerations. Some poststructuralists and localists would probably think that it also illustrates the indeterminacy of the social world and the dynamic nature of situation-specific action and the employment of linguistic resources for making claims in these. But one may also say that financial results and client-perceived quality seem to be important and that although core objectives or values may be difficult to rank, it appears that for persons working as senior consultants, in charge of specific projects, these are more significant than values such as workplace democracy or job satisfaction in this firm. The latter are also moral virtues and may be used to signal the right impression. The interview indicates that the consultancy world needs to deal with issues surrounding making clients happy, doing things that signal seriousness and a sensitivity to client considerations. It also points to a tendency to cut corners, when this is likely to be undetected, in order to make a plan and keep to the budget. It is likely that this is an indicator of how the firm actually operates in many situations, as there are no particular reasons to assume that the interviewee has a political reason for claiming this nor that he should be ignorant about it. In the interview excerpt discussed here he hardly expresses a positive identity or does much successful impression management. I don't think he adapts to a norm for how one talks about the subject with an organization studies researcher, etc. Claims about not cheating are more dubious as truth claims than statements that we sometimes 'cheat', as the former more than the latter can be understood as an effect of social mechanisms guiding people to produce a specific type of answer.[4]

The interview does seem to have some value as an indicator of some aspects of practices and meanings of consultancy work in this specific type of firm. It points to the importance for consultants to work flexibly around and with issues of being (or appearing as) client oriented and keeping to budget, expressing 'quality as absolutely the most important' (and probably buying into this in many situations) and then being prepared to modify or bypass this and work pragmatically and cost-efficiently in those respects where the centrality of quality is less obvious or easy to assess. In this sense we can, perhaps, after some careful thinking through of various ways of interpreting the interview arrive at a position where a set of reasonably well grounded interpretations can be made. Of course this is only one step in the entire research process – but it is a vital one and all empirical material needs to be carefully scrutinized before deciding to make bold claims about moving beyond the studying of interview talk as such.

Conclusion

In this chapter I have argued for a reflexive pragmatism approach to the research interview, which means the employment of a variety of supplementary perspectives and lines of interpretation on interviews. (The idea is of course equally relevant for considering other types of research and empirical material, but the focus here is on the interview). Two partly opposing principles are here combined. Reflexivity is defined as an inclination to try a set of various interpretations and challenge one's favourite discourses with alternative metaphors and lines of reasoning, producing a variety of possibilities and considerations. Here it is important both to be 'defensive' or 'disciplinary', acknowledging the problems and disadvantages with a specific interpretation/ claim of capturing something (a truth) *and* being 'offensive', coming up with creative re-interpretations and imagining more than one interesting opportunity for saying something. I refer to these as elements of D- and R-reflexivity respectively. The interplay between these is important, where challenging/undermining one representation and/or interpretation encourages a re-representation and re-interpretation. Making the reader aware of uncertainties with and alternatives to the favoured interpretation may be one positive contribution.

Exercises investigating rigour and alternative interpretations need to be balanced with a concern to get something interesting and important out of the study. Pragmatic considerations mean that often something reasonably well supported and valuable as a step on the knowledge-creation process can be used in a project. Good reasons need to be mobilized before seeing interviews as indicative of experiences or behaviours out there, but one can't ask for any final or foolproof evidence that this is more than just interview talk. Sometimes it may be enough to demonstrate that an interview statement may be equally plausible as being indicative of such 'outside-the-interview' phenomena as local construction work, if this allows for an interesting and important research contribution. Here it is important that researchers are open about this, as well as in the final research text, and that s/he encourages the reader also to be reflexive, e.g. in considering alternative interpretations. This is then different from the normal research practice of presenting a number of seemingly coherent interview quotations – often picked and framed to create a highly persuasive text – and then placing the reader in a passive position, as a consumer who is supposed to just accept the 'evidence' demonstrated before them.

Notes

1 This section draws upon Alvesson et al. (2008).
2 This is not to deny that the sets of practices include some elements of both: destabilizing practices can offer some sort of alternative understanding – even Foucauldian ideas on how knowledge produces rather than reveals truth say something about how subjects are created; in the case of multi-perspective practices, there is frequently a partial or minimalist deconstruction when one perspective is used to disturb another (Alvesson, 2002).
3 This can to some extent be tested through varying the scene in interviews: vary interviewers, frame the research project differently, switch between different physical sites for the interview, etc.
4 This is not to say that we should not be open also towards what may appear as 'non-moral' statements being guided by social norms. People may feel that in order to appear 'honest' some confessions about not-so-nice behaviour on their behalf are necessary. Or that a lot of impression management needs to be compensated for with some talk presenting the interviewee in a less flattering way. In order to trick the researcher to accept some politically motivated claims as 'true', some talk in which the interviewee appears as a person not particularly politically manipulating at all may preceed and/or follow truth-claims supportive of the interviewee and his/her group's political interests. Still, I think the assessment of the interview above is reasonable and allows for sufficient grounding to take the 'truth-aspect' seriously, about both how the interview relates to the situation and, based on that, what practices sometimes look like.

7

IMPLICATIONS FOR RESEARCH
PRACTICE

The kind of thinking suggested by understanding(s) of the research interview here proposed can be used in at least four different ways:

1 Revising and improving research practice.
2 Increasing the rigor and carefulness of interpretations of interviews.
3 Reconsidering the kinds of research questions we can ask.
4 Acknowledging the limits of rigorous empirical work and the use of empirical studies for non-descriptive purposes.

All this aims to reduce being a victim of taken-for-granted assumptions and established wisdom in interview-based research and to counter naïvety when dealing with claims on how to capture reality, and also to increase the chances of being more theoretically inspired, reflexive and creative in research. This may sound too ambitious, perhaps even arrogant, but I think that some effects in these two directions can be accomplished through the framework advocated in this book.

Implications for methodological practice and technique

Qualifying the thinking about method by incorporating a set of various reference points – as exemplified by the eight metaphors – may encourage more informed ways of fieldwork. There is a rich variety of ideas in the literature on how to practically conduct interviews and sometimes authors will recommend opposing techniques. This is sometimes the case also within the same overall approach, e.g. among authors interested in interviews aiming to arrive at deep statements of people's authentic experiences. Here the ideal sometimes is for the researcher to avoid getting involved in conversations and expressing personal views ('it's your opinion that is important') and sometimes doing so in such order to engage and open up the interviewee ('I myself feel sometimes like ...'). Romantics would thus diverge whether an interviewer should try to make an interviewee take centre stage or come to the fore as active and engage participant in the talk.

As I mentioned earlier I am skeptical of any general advice on how best to do an interview. I don't think there is such a thing as one best way of doing interviews, even if one can specify the overall type of knowledge one is after (facts, meanings or discourse), so even within, say, romanticism, it is difficult to claim a set of rules for how to do it. Perhaps a very inexperienced and uncertain interviewer could start with picking a recommended approach and then gradually rethinking this, if and when it seems worthwhile. My interest is less in providing pointers than in offering an overall way of reasoning that can support and encourage a critical awareness of the problems and possibilities of interviewing. Such an awareness may mean that one can make situation-specific interpretations and interventions that will reduce some problems. Crucial here is thinking through the issues beforehand, being sensitive to what is happening in the interview situation and then learning from one interview what may happen and being prepared for dealing with 'complications' in subsequent interviews. Here I am assuming that an interviewer is not interested in studying local interaction and interview talk, but wants to use the interview for saying something about other phenomena. This means that the primary interest of the researcher is *not* to study how the interviewee tries to build up a credible and coherent story, is being subjugated to and spoken by a discourse (producing a specific version of the individual) or is doing impression management. The researcher therefore has some interest in counteracting these logics dominating the interview talk. There are never any guarantees for success in this respect – it is after all very much up to the interviewee – but some interventions may be productive.

Interview interventions

An awareness of script-following may, if one is not interested in studying that aspect, for example lead to interview interventions in which familiar, institutionalized ways of talking about things are discouraged. Questions or comments such as, 'Can you explore that with other words?' or 'I have the feeling that conventionally used words in this area really don't capture things that well', when interviewees use standard jargon, may trigger responses that are less caught up with script-coherent expressions. Other interventions may signal that it is ok and appreciated if 'political correctness' does not dominate the talk or that is not a good idea to use official expressions when describing something, though this must obviously be expressed so that the interviewee does not feel offended. In relation to the example of the senior manager (citation from Watson at the end of Chapter 5), an encouragement to use other words than 'engineering-led' and 'market-led' culture may be a possibility. The interviewer may more explicitly encourage the interviewee to approach the subject matter from a different angle by introducing or changing vocabularies: one may for example ask about co-ordination, power, hierarchy, subordination or managerial work instead of, or in addition to, leadership. Or one could ask questions regarding the centrality of engineering knowledge and then encourage the interviewee to discuss various forms of competences, their significance in the organization and what kind of changes may be motivated. Doing re-starts and coming back to a particular theme via different vocabularies (points of entry) at later stages in an interview may be useful. Similarly, the researcher can change the scene for an interaction by becoming more or less romantic (emphasizing the genuine human encounter through being more personally involved).

The interviewer can also try to modify interviewees' assumptions by presenting the project in various ways to different interviewees. If the researcher consciously and explicitly positions him/herself and the research project in different ways, then he/she will get some understanding of how (or if) framing matters. This can be done either for the same interviewee subject – adding more and different information in the middle of the interview – or for different subjects in a 'sample'. This may allow for investigating how different kinds of assumptions or framed contexts for interviews can affect the accounts produced. This would mean that the storyline and the mini-paradigm developed by the interviewee of what this is all about may be revised: the researcher then becomes less of a victim of how the interviewee tries to make sense of the project and the specific questions asked. Jorgenson (1991), in her study of understandings of 'families' for example, could have presented herself as a 'research psychologist', a 'family expert' and 'soon-to-become-parent-for-the-first-time'. Parker (2000), studying organizations, could have emphasized his youth, his expertise, his pro- or anti-management orientations in presentations and in the questions asked/comments made, and then seen if and how the responses varied. This may be seen as manipulation but I don't think there is any significant ethical problem involved here. Most interviewers and research projects are not one-dimensional in their identities and orientations and can 'honestly' express self-images and project purposes in different ways. And all forms of interviewing will include an element of mild manipulation.

Other themes as indicated by the eight metaphors (or in other ways to be seen as playing an uncertain role in the interview) can also be addressed in similar ways: Interviewees' identity positionings can, for example, be investigated by addressing them through various identities (you, as a manager, subordinate, peer, woman, Christian, very experienced/old …) and discourses. The political interest of interviewees may be reduced if the researcher communicates that the research will *not* be reported back to decision makers in the organization or policy makers, nor is expected to reach the mass media. This may reduce politically guided interview accounts but also decrease the motivation of people to participate – as with all techniques, this is a mixed blessing. Working with these re-framings of the research and the researcher, varying the vocabulary and identity communication, may make the interview situation more complicated and stressful for the participants, but may reduce talk guided by specific scripts or assumptions. At a minimum the researcher may be in a better position to assess critically the effects of particular languages and assumptions on the interview responses.

This kind of implication for research practice would, however, mean a relatively modest lesson in the rethinking of the interview leading to some strengthening of neo-positivist and romantic views on interviewing. The possibilities of 'rationalizing' interview practice, of translating a theoretical understanding into a set of practical and technical ideas, are limited.

Supplementary interviewees

Sometimes it makes good sense to interview people other than the key group where this is possible. If people in the targeted category (immigrant housewives, crime victims, parents, retired people, lawyers …) seem to produce certain accounts of their experiences and situations, then perhaps people 'around' them can be approached for supplementary (alternative/verifying) material, for example friends, relatives, offenders, neighbours, clients, etc. may be interviewed. People supplementing material may be less well informed of the topics of which the housewives, victims, lawyers, etc. are 'experts' (their own experiences), but may offer interesting input on what interview questions one could raise with the target group and facilitate an interpretation of their responses.

Sometimes using supplementary interviewees who will allow for accumulating material of even more direct bearing on the 'key' or targeted person or group is possible. Hollway and Jefferson (2000) interviewed not only Ron, a British young man with a long criminal history, about his relationship to crime, but also, 'at the same time in the same house', Ron's best friend, Craig, 'who shares many of his criminal exploits' (p. 130). (The two researchers interviewed one subject each.) This enabled triangulation, i.e. increase reliability through using rich and varied material. Of course, both interviews may be influenced by elements of moral storytelling and adaption to the specific social setting, but the material is considerably stronger than if the study relied only on one case person, Ron. One could of course have imagined even more interviews about Ron, with people from social welfare, police, relatives, neighbours, victims, etc., but interviews with the two allowed much richer material to appear than is common in studies of this phenomenon.

In general, I have the feeling that many interview researchers could work harder and more creatively in order to get access to more viewpoints and richer material by using a better variety of interviewees. It is often too easy to focus only on people in an easily identified group. Also, if the studies address identity or other 'subjective' aspects people around the targeted case subjects could be asked to give their views. Thomas and Davies (2005) for example studied the subjective resistance of some people in public sector to reforms (i.e. resisting norms for how one should think and be as a person in a regime of 'New Public Management'), relying solely on interviews with the persons supposedly experiencing themselves as resisting, but it could have been of more interest if the interviewees' talk suggesting them being critical and non-compliant would have been supported by the impressions of people around them at work. Indications of resistance only coming out in the interview setting – where people in interviews with academics may want to come across as skeptical and autonomous – is perhaps of less interest than if other people around the subject could notice at least some signs of such resistance. This is not easy as the focus is on subjectivity and not behaviour, but something of the former may be expressed (ironic comments, sighs, negative facial expressions) as well and may be detected by people around the person producing a resisting subjectivity. If people close to a focal person indicating resistance in an interview, only notes compliance, then the relevance of the resistance talk in the interview seems debateable.

Supplementing interviews with participant observations

One major implication of the uncertainties of interviews would of course be to rely less on interviews than on ethnographic work, in which not only interviews with a variety of people but also even more so participant observations are central (Hammersley & Atkinson, 1994). A major advantage would be to get broader and more varied empirical material as interviews and observations typically cover partly different phenomena. There are good reasons for a move in qualitative work from being primarily interview-based to becoming more ethnographic. However, participant observation is very time-consuming and many interesting research questions call for capturing the voices and experiences of those targeted for understanding. In addition interviews are an important part of most ethnographies, so this approach also calls for deep thinking about how to handle interview situations and accounts. Doing interviews as part of an ethnography has some advantages compared with doing only interviews. If the researcher 'has been there' for some time it may de-mystify the interview situation, facilitate communication, give the researcher a better pre-understanding and perhaps make interviewees less inclined to engage in political action or impression management. So apart from being less reliant on interviews, ethnographic work may also reduce some of the problems described here.

Sometimes well-picked research tasks will allow for a good interplay between interviews and observations in terms of increasing rigor. Ulver-Sneistrup (2008), for example, studied how people related to status aspects of consumption and focused on home and home aesthetics. By conducting interviews in respondents' homes and observing these skilfully, observations added to interviews, made it possible to improve these, and also to do some checking of the interview responses.

Thinking about how interviews work (and don't work) during the entire research process

Irrespective if interview work is combined with 'hanging around' or not, it is important to consider on an on-going basis what the interviews seem to be about and any possible problems that may emerge – given a researcher's hopes and intentions. Learning and reflection are vital, as it is difficult to predict what is happening or rely on recommendations and recipes in the normative method literature for how to do interviews. Of course, we can always suspect that political correctness and other social scripts will play a role in research on, for example, equal opportunity, ethnicity or discrimination and that people in senior positions in society may be politically aware. But we can't take this for granted and in most other situations unexpected issues may appear. Therefore, in addition to carefully considering things in advance and during interviews, it is vital to look closely at a set of interviews after they have been conducted and let the insights inform one's considerations and interpretive sensitivity during subsequent interviews.

Implications for a more rigorous and reflexive approach to use interview material for 'conventional' purposes

A challenge for the vast majority of interview-based research concerns the options of using the empirical material for studies to go beyond just investigating interview talk or people's use of conversational skills. A skeptic may ask an interview researcher 'What have you studied?' and then ironically translate the response 'Yes, talk in interviews'. The only thing we can know for sure is what people say when we interview them, similar to knowing that the only thing questionnaires can tell us is which boxes respondents have put their X's in. We need to bear in mind that the research interview is a rather artificial situation where in most cases two strangers meet and one is supposed to produce data for the other. But can it mean more than that? That the researcher feels that the interviewee seems trustworthy and has faith in people is fine, but this may say more about naïve assumptions by researchers and interviewees' skills in impression management than anything else. So what are researchers to do?

In the literature, there are many good ideas about strengthening the credibility of interview-based research. Kvale talks about validity – he does not refer to correspondence with an objective reality but to 'defensible knowledge claims' – and suggests that this is

> … ascertained by examining the sources of invalidity. The stronger falsification attempts a proposition has survived, the more valid, the more trustworthy the knowledge. Validation comes to depend on the quality of craftsmanship during investigation, continually checking, questioning, and theoretically interpreting the findings. (1996: 241)

The approach advocated in this book is to refine the ability to critically interpret interview material and consider the logics or processes informing its production. One option would be to maintain conventional concerns – using interviews as pipelines for studying other settings or phenomena than talk and interaction in the interview situation (as a location of discourses, as a scene, as a site of political action, identity work, etc.) – but then to more carefully try to evaluate the nature of the empirical material in light of the metaphor framework proposed. Empirical material that withstands the onslaught of critical scrutiny, i.e. does not seem to be best understood through any or several of the 'anti-tool' metaphors, can then be used in a conventional way. Experiences, meanings, behaviours, events, etc. can then, in principle, be targeted.

One possibility is here to consider both the 'how' and 'what' aspects of the interview, where the former refers to the conversational and other interaction-specific, local elements and the latter to what can be carved out as indicators of experiences or representations of practices or situations 'outside' the interview context (Holstein & Gubrium, 1997). It then becomes possible to substantiate the case for using it in order to make statements about phenomena 'out there' (outside the interview situation). In the conventional view of empirical material the interviewee is assumed to have provided the researcher with reliable data about a phenomenon, as long as there are no apparent reasons to believe otherwise. At least the rules for coding and conventions for presentation of data would generally imply this kind of stance. A more reflexive approach would replace this assumption with one of skepticism, but not of rejection. It would assume that there is a lot more than truth-telling involved (as suggested above), but that these other elements or 'logics' do not necessarily dominate. It is only if it can be credibly argued that specific interview accounts have validity beyond the local context, beyond the reproduction of discourse, etc. and indicate something 'out there' that statements can be treated in this way. Just presenting quotations as evidence (for something outside interview talk) is then insufficient: crucial here is making a strong case for why one should accept that the talk indicates the phenomenon the interviewee is talking about.

If accounts deviate from scripts/moral storytelling elements, if they cannot be explained in terms of political interest or efforts to avoid embarrassment through putting together a reasonably coherent talk, etc., then they can perhaps be seen as strong indicators of how an interviewee experiences the focused social world. But this needs to be thought

IMPLICATIONS FOR RESEARCH PRACTICE

through and shown – for example, by comparing the plausibility of this kind of interpretation to the alternatives presented in this book. This can be done intuitively, which is less credible, or more systematically and carefully. The ideas for more reflexively informed interview practices discussed in the previous section are helpful here, as they allow for exploring the relevance of some of the metaphors in understanding interview talk and how it seems to be a response to various inputs, including the social and linguistic contingencies of the interview situation.

To combine interviews with observations is often, as was mentioned above, a good move as it can broaden and enrich studies and also make it easier to ask good questions in interviews. But sometimes the trustworthiness of interview material can also be strengthened through observational material, although it is normally not possible to directly compare or 'hone in on' results emerging from different methods, due to variations in the context (Denzin, 1994; Potter & Wetherell, 1987). In other cases interviews with a variety of people – having different political interests, identifying construction projects, etc. – may support the validity (credibility) of the interview material. (The rules of hermeneutical research for assessing the value of sources are very relevant here, although seemingly underutilized in the interview literature; see Alvesson & Sköldberg, 2009, Chapter 4).

The point here is that it is insufficient just to present, or refer to, a number of interview accounts or the use of a particular tactic in managing interviewees in order to claim trustworthiness. A normal tactic is to emphasize the quantity of the empirical material and the technical rules for coding this. A large and varied empirical material may facilitate informed judgement and using rules and techniques for data management are sometimes practical, but there is a risk that large volumes and a reliance on technical procedures may draw attention away from, and reduce the time and energy for, reflexive interpretation. It may also give a misleading impression of robustness. Interview reports from several people are not necessarily an indication of high validity: this may indicate that they followed the same script or engaged in similar impression management tactics.

Let us go back to the example discussed earlier (see the end of Chapter 5 and the manager cited by Watson, 1994), where the importance of a change from an engineering-led to a market-led culture was emphasized. I previously addressed how intervention techniques could reduce the uncertainty of what was actually happening in an interview. These have a strong relevance for the chances of understanding the interview and using it for conventional purposes. A case for relying upon the interview as an indicator of the interviewee's experiences and/ or 'objective' phenomena about the corporation would be strengthened *if* a set of interviewee accounts triggered by the use of different entrances in the interview would broadly point in a similar direction. So if for example the researcher, perhaps later on in the interview, would ask about the significance of engineering knowledge and the interviewee would perhaps acknowledge this but still come back to the issue of insufficient market knowledge or considerations, it may be read as a small indication that the statements were saying something about that person's meanings or even about the 'objective' corporate situation. In the best of worlds, observations on the topic would be called for but broad issues such as the underlying cultural meanings of a village or a tribe may be difficult to directly observe, although an ambitious ethnographic study may be able to throw some light on this.

An increased emphasis on rigor and an expectation that the researcher should demonstrate why and how the interview material indicated the 'truth' (experiences or practices outside the interview context) would most likely mean a drastic reduction in the scope of studies and claims made in the currently dominating type of interview-based research. Many studies and many uses of interview statements would have difficulties in withstanding the critical pummeling suggested here.

Implications for novel research question and new lines of interpretation

A third possible implication is to let our awareness of the (im)possibilities of various uses of interview material influence the research question asked. We can't just adapt a method to the objective of research, instead an a priori or gradually developing methodological awareness should also influence and revise the objective. Sometimes the latter will be initially informed by an instrument or human encounter view that subsequently can be seen to not hold water after close scrutiny i.e. if interviewee talk doesn't seem to reflect 'facts' or 'true experiences'. Research questions then need to be reconsidered. The reconceptualizations of interviews suggested in the book offering a variety of lines of interpretation of interview material can thus trigger changes in research agendas at various stages of the research process, and sometimes also at a later stage. This appears especially

IMPLICATIONS FOR RESEARCH PRACTICE

worthwhile as it is clear that many research projects relying on interviews will have great difficulties in showing that interview accounts can be read credibly as indicating some phenomena that are grounded in a reality – or experiences/meanings thereof – outside of the interview situation. This may become apparent to a researcher fairly late on in the process, after a closer look at the empirical material produced (gathered). However, making a late revision is better than sticking to a naïve idea and trying to deliver this with, for the stated purpose, shaky material. An emerging awareness of the problems of rigor can thus to some extent be dealt with by revising the research purpose in order to close the gap between the purpose and those (credible) empirical results that can actually be delivered.

Raising demands on rigor and credibility will limit the scope of studies and research topics to be investigated by interviews. Recognizing the futility of many conventional research tasks may trigger a re-orientation of research. There is no point in asking questions that simply can't be reliably answered through empirical inquiry. We can here point to the linguistic turn(s) in social science and philosophy (Alvesson & Kärreman, 2000a; Rosenau, 1992) to remind ourselves of problems going far beyond language use in our claims to knowledge. As language is hardly best seen as a medium for reflecting or mirroring reality (either out there or inner states of mind), but a discourse, used to construct versions of reality and where meaning is local, metaphorical and performative, the difficulties in using interviews as simple (or even complicated) pipelines to phenomena outside this discourse are tremendous. The problems this points to for moving far outside language should not be underestimated. But this does not mean that some wellgrounded moves to go some, perhaps modest way beyond the interview context, are impossible (Alvesson & Kärreman, 2000a).

Interviews can thus be conducted but the interpretation should be careful about the 'distance' between the phenomenon one tries to study and the interview as an empirical situation. This means that one can use the interview as a productive site for studying phenomena which are not that dissimilar from the interview situation, i.e. the use of certain discourses. This would go beyond localism, but cautiously. Important here then is coming up with research questions that don't call for breathtaking leaps, from moving from interview talk to making bold claims about completely different phenomena – family life, school experiences, attitudes to immigrants, fear of crime, etc. All eight proposed metaphors for interviews can offer potentially interesting ways to use interview material with more care than is usual.

It may be impossible for example, to investigate which motives are 'really' central for people. We may never know whether interviewees really know their motives, whether they really are trying to tell us about their 'real' motives or whether they are have been verbally successful in doing so. The burdens put on interviewees to tell even the subjective truth are high. Yet so are those on the researcher to sort out this and decide how to interpret the material. Interview material may, however, throw some light on vocabularies of motives (Mills, 1940). This might perhaps be seen as trivial, but it is not. Such vocabularies are central elements in how reality is being constructed, how people express and adapt (or resist) norms should be central concerns, e.g. for how they navigate in social settings, form identities, etc. People in different occupations, classes, age groups, genders and organizations may produce different talk about motives.

Of course, it is then important to give good reasons, and/or some indications, for talk during interviews saying something about talk in everyday life or in public or semi-public settings – family or pub talk, service encounters at hotels, union-management negotiation situations. This link between interview talk and talk in other situations can't be assumed. People will talk differently for different audiences on different occasions. As Boje (1991) has argued, interviews about stories (storytelling) in workplaces may give a rather different impression from studying (observing) storytelling in 'real life' – here the performance of storytelling and the specific context and readings of the listeners are vital aspects. Recapitulating how one tells stories – about executives, workers, customers, episodes – to colleagues or subordinates in live situations may be difficult. The same is so with references to motives and motivation. Interview talk then may have an uncertain relationship with how stories are told and motives are talked about, with many important aspects being lost. The dynamics of the situation are very important to appreciate in order to understand how stories and motives are expressed and how they work. Still, some key elements of the stories being told and the motivation vocabulary in circulation (expressing values, appealing to the imagination, giving cognitive clues to understanding how things work, etc.) may be reproduced reasonably well in an interview. It is much easier to communicate something reliable about the stories people tell and the motives they emphasize, than to say something about one's decision making, values,

IMPLICATIONS FOR RESEARCH PRACTICE

attitudes to immigrants, feelings for one's parents or something else that is not primarily a linguistic or discursive phenomenon and that also may be very personally sensitive. This does not mean that there are not problems and uncertainties also about studying communication phenomena through interviews as well, such as telling of storytelling or expressions of motives – people may be selective or polish their stories or expressions of motives (only telling politically correct ones), choose stories or motives that one thinks a researcher may understand or be interested in, etc. So critical interpretations are also necessary here. However, communication phenomena are typically more researchable in interviews than for example feelings, values or motives. And while a lot of the dynamics around storytelling and vocabularies of motives in action can be easily lost, some of the key features of stories and other forms of language use that interviewees report in interviews may allow for interesting investigations.

The accounts by two senior consultants in my examples in the beginning of Chapter 5 and the end of Chapter 6 could productively be explored as organizational discourse (or in any of the other ways suggested by the brief metaphor-based interpretation above). Complemented with a richer empirical material, these could illuminate how organizational life is permeated with hierarchy and market talk, client-oriented quality emphasis and ideals about working smartly to stick to the calculation and meet the budget and how these themes are used in interactive, persuasive contexts and related to issues of power, legitimacy, leadership, espoused values, etc., with all this understood mainly within a discursive context. These kinds of talk may be more or less loosely (or tightly) related to what people think, feel and value as well as what they do in various everyday life situations and what 'really' characterizes the organization and profession. But this is hard to tell. Interview-based research does not easily allow any conclusions here, so care is recommended in making statements about (stable or common) practices or values and cognitions in firms. Yet the circulation of these discourses are possible salient ingredients in organizational life and thus are important themes in how organizations function.

Another example of how interview talk can be cautiously related to other, but not too 'distant' (different) themes concerns some aspects of self-construction taking place in the interview, with some potential bearing on extra-interview settings. Grey, in a study of junior professionals in a big accounting firm, asked first-year trainees about the need to appear enthusiastic when performing tedious audit tasks, and got answers such as the following:

> I'm not saying it's always interesting but I always know that I'm doing it for myself, in the end, because it's getting me a qualification I can do anything with. So I don't think 'this is really boring', I think 'this is getting me to where I want to be'. (1994: 487)

This account may be read as *not* mirroring the feelings and thinking of the interview as actually constructing a particular form of subjectivity, defined through the career project. This discursive act – whether espoused or produced in a mute dialogue that the subject has with her or himself – is then part of a particular project. The interview situation and identity-creating talk performed thus does not refer to 'something else', such as a fixed attitude or a career strategy, but can be seen as an instance of the on-going project of 'getting me where I want to be'; it is one of a myriad of micro-events in which the subject tells her or himself and others that this is not primarily boring but a career project. This does not prevent contradictory experiences and meanings. This kind of interpretation – well in line with Grey's approach – then reduces the gap between the interview situation as an empirical example and the speculative more of going beyond this and refer to something broader and 'extra-situational'. The question of whether that interviewee 'really' sees the work as not boring or is truly career-oriented is then avoided. The 'mobilization' or self-persuasion of himself along the outlined trajectory is what takes place, both in the interview and possibly in other settings.

Important here for reflexive research is thus to be hesitant in moving too 'far away' from the character of what actually is the key ingredient: interview talk. Finding research questions that are in line with the empirical material and do not put unrealistic and naïve burdens on this material is then crucial. This may mean a 'retreat to' or concentration on 'interview-like' issues, e.g. certain discursive acts (effect-oriented talk). This may call for a considerable rethink on the part of the researcher regarding what a project is all about and what can actually be delivered as a credible empirical study. Arguably, such a rethink will often mean a move from romanticism or neo-positivism to taking localist ideas more seriously, but the argument of this book is that we must also balance rigor with relevance and that reflexive sophistication should be combined with pragmatic considerations. A 'safe' and data-close interpretation can easily lead to trivial results. And sometimes a

IMPLICATIONS FOR RESEARCH PRACTICE

researcher may start with localism-inspired understandings but the interview interactions and responses may encourage other, perhaps less 'local' research possibilities. Seeing and using the interview as a site for communicating interviewees' experiences and knowledge should not be excluded.

Side-stepping description: using interviews for idea-generation and analysis

Another possible implication here is to acknowledge the problems of empirical work and the notorious uncertainty of data and then use all of this more loosely, as an input to the generation of ideas and the fine-tuning of reasoning. This means that one must put less emphasis on the details of empirical material, at least in terms of ambitious description. The basic position of this book – as in almost all writings on interviews – is in how to use empirical work in a sophisticated and ambitious way. A description of the empirical object targeted for study is vital here. Most researchers using interviews will be eager to produce good descriptions and I have followed this ambition in the book. But sometimes interesting research questions and strong theoretical ideas do not play well with what we are able to study empirically. Perhaps we should be more prepared to let the data abdicate from their privileged position? This is of course not an issue solely for interview-based studies but for all forms of social research. According to Astley (1985) a theory's influence will have very little to do with the degree of empirical support it has received. Gergen and Gergen (1991), taking the idea that language cannot mirror reality seriously and arguing that consequently there cannot be a 'fit' between theory and data, suggested that empirical work can be used for generating valuable vocabularies that are useful for understanding but no more than that. I don't think we should go so far as to marginalize the role of empirical work, but perhaps we should be more modest about empirical claims in many cases, realizing that interviewees' shoulders are not vast and the capacities of interview talk to mirror or say something valid about reality are limited. Can we, for example, during interviews over one or two hours seriously expect managers to give an account of their 'leadership' that actually reflects parts of their work days and certain qualities of their relations with others? Or is it realistic to assume that parents can describe and/or explain their relationships with their children in fairly brief talks with strangers?[1] It is possible that a careful methodological reflection on what interviews (as well as other practices) can do for example should occasionally limit our hubris and encourage the use of empirical material for inspirational or illustrative purposes or as an ambiguous corrective for bad ideas, rather than provide a robust basis for a determination of the truth or the development of (grounded) theory. Accepting this view would liberate our thinking from empiricist strait-jackets, but of course also limit the options for making strong empirical claims.

One could then conduct interviews for other purposes than producing valid descriptions. Interview material could be used in order to generate ideas, provide illustrations or to give correctives for theoretical ideas that do not seem to be useful to our understanding. Providing researchers with a degree of sensitivity for the social reality they are interested in could be valuable for theoretical work. This may be valuable even if the feeling for this reality is not as exact or grounded as believers in the knowledge- and understanding-transmitting capacity of interviews would suggest.

A somewhat different approach would be to use more fully the knowledge and skills of those interviewed and enrol them less for descriptive than for analytical and theoretical work. One can try to use interviews in order to investigate how things hang together and what alternative social arrangements are possible. This is sometimes called the analytical interview (Kreiner & Mouritsen, 2005). Here an interviewee is mobilized not as a respondent or even an informant being asked to tell how things are or how they experience themselves and their reality, but as an analyst aiding the researcher in explanations for the current state of affairs and in exploring potentials.

A possible metaphor for this interview could be the interview as a mini-seminar. Jackall (1988) also used many of his informants for analytical purposes. He produced cases – based on descriptive interviews – focused on managers and professionals in business who faced moral problems. He then presented these to a group of managers who were not involved in the specific cases and asked them to comment upon what had happened, something which greatly benefitted his analysis. This goes slightly outside the interview as normally defined but indicates how one can use interview material in talk with informants who have been mobilized for analytical purposes.

Another example of moving away from a strong belief in the robustness of empirical material and the possibility of making empirical claims is suggested by Alvesson and Kärreman (2011), who were working with a broad strategy for theory development that was not specifically focused on but also highly relevant for interview-based studies. Here it is suggested that empirical studies should be seen as a matter of considering alternative constructions with the aim of choosing those with the greatest potential for challenging existing ideas and theories and developing new theory. Rather than building blocks offering the solid ground for theoretical ideas, empirical material is viewed as a critical dialogue partner. The criteria for a good interview would then be not whether the phenomenon gets addressed in a 'correct' way, but whether there is the capacity to trigger rethinking and creativity on behalf of the researcher. The emphasis is thus moved away from descriptive precision to idea-generative power, although a reasonably (rather than optimal) high degree of rigor and trustworthiness on the descriptive side is also called for.

My point here of course is not that we should give up conventional empirical purposes, but that sometimes we should consider that what we can actually say based on interviews (and also other empirical material) may be less than we want, and that other, not so 'empirically constrained' research ambitions may be upgraded. One can still undertake ambitious empirical work, but that it is in itself mainly a springboard for doing something different – work with ideas, concepts and theories transcending what it is possible to ground or substantiate empirically.

Summary

In order for interview accounts to be used in conventional ways – seen as mirroring exterior or interior reality – it is reasonable to expect researchers to make credible that a knowledge-producing logic dominates accounts and that the social reality out there or the meanings and experiences of interviewees put strong imprints on these. The accounts should preferably *not* be best interpreted based on the eight metaphors suggested here. This may be read as rather tough demands on conventional research, having implications, of course, not only for interviews but also for other research practices (such as diaries and questionnaire responses). Compared to some views expressed by localists, the approach suggested here still gives more space for using interviews in order to gather empirical material on people's meanings, experiences or social practices. Rather than predefining any interview content as for example being tightly connected (only) to the local situation and/or following scripts or drawing upon cultural resources in order to build a particular moral order (Baker, 1997; Silverman, 1993, 2006), one could critically examine an account for such elements and evaluate to what extent these are significant. Arguably, this is not always the case and interviews can then be used for other purposes than those envisioned by localist research programmes.

Such critical assessments could lead to four responses, as were addressed in this chapter.

1 Revising and improving research *practice*.
2 Increasing the rigor and carefulness of *interpretations* of interviews.
3 Reconsidering the kinds of *research questions* we can ask.
4 Acknowledging the limits of rigorous empirical work and the use of empirical studies for *idea-generation* and other non-descriptive purposes.

These are to some extent complementary and interchangeable. If a researcher is successful in working with some of the social, linguistic and political complexities of the interview then this can reinforce the case for using interview statements in fairly ambitious ways in terms of description, in line with conventional purposes. Careful interpretation of the empirical material can then perhaps easier convince the researcher and an audience that the material can stand the scrutiny of reflexive interpretations in which other logics than 'knowledge-transmission' are taken seriously. Such rigor may mean also that conventional, in relationship to localists, often much broader research questions can be dealt with. On the other side, a willingness and capacity to take seriously the limitation of interview talk may encourage research questions that are more methodologically thought through and realistic. The research interview can't always or even typically carry the burden, even with reflexive interventions, of reporting truthfully on people's meanings (inner self, sense-making, experiences) or the social practices or events that they have observed/participated in. This would imply that sometimes not even careful reflexive interventions in interview work or strict and rigorous interpretations will allow for strong empirical claims. Simply finding research questions in tune with what is actually studied – talk in social settings – makes the research project in certain key respects much less complicated and more convincing. But of course the responsibility to come up with something interesting and also to ground the study in a certain degree of reflexivity still lies with the researcher. And problems of a possibly too

IMPLICATIONS FOR RESEARCH PRACTICE

narrow domain and doubtful relevance may still haunt them, as many research tasks around talking, interacting, using vocabularies, relating to social norms, etc. may still be seen as not as socially important as conventional research projects that addresses facts and/or meanings – themes that often are perceived as more socially valuable and significant than 'just talk'. The fourth possible implication – downplaying empirical description and using interviews for idea-generating and analytical purposes – may be more in line with expectations of offering significant, broadly relevant research results, but coming up with a theoretical contribution is often more demanding than empirical description, so it is not necessarily an easy way out of methodological-empirical difficulties.

Note

1 This comment is, of course, even more valid regarding questionnaire research (Alvesson & Deetz, 2000).

8

CONCLUSION

Recent developments in philosophy and social theory have encouraged new lines of thinking in relation to methodology. Problems of representation, the nature of language, the centrality of paradigms, the inseparability of researcher and knowledge, as well as problems and options of writing, have received much attention (e.g. Alvesson & Deetz, 2000; Alvesson & Sköldberg, 2009; Denzin, 1997; Denzin & Lincoln, 1994; Kilduff & Mehra, 1997; Silverman, 2006; Van Maanen, 1995). Relatively little of this has specifically addressed interviews, but rather has dealt with the problems of describing reality on a more general level. There is often a gap or disconnection between more intellectual reasoning on methodology and the specific work on research practices. This is unfortunate. Most authors on interviews, although signalling some awareness of a far-reaching critique of conventional research projects, including qualitative work aspiring to reveal meaning (experiences, values, sense making, identities …), have retained, as Fontana and Frey (2005) describe it, a 'conservative' interest in description. Empirical claims are, despite some expression of caution and recognition of uncertainty, still fairly strong.

Apart from the critique from (what is here referred to as) localist authors, writings on interviews tend to be normatively and technically oriented and weak on theory and reflexivity. Dominant understandings of interviews encircle around a metaphor of the interview as a tool or, to minor extent, a knowledge-creating human encounter and the outcome of the skilful use of it is a pipeline to the interiors of interviewees or the exteriors of social reality. The issue is 'how to obtain reliable and valid knowledge of the social world through the various views of the interacting subjects' (Kvale, 1996: 7). That many researchers emphasize the 'softer' aspects of this tool view and the need to use it flexibly and consider the role of the researcher does not prevent them from, at the end of the day (when the journal or book manuscript is to be submitted), relying on interviews as tools for accessing social reality. By utilizing the right theoretical idea and technique researchers think they can reach the facts or meanings aimed for. Hollway and Jefferson (2000: 37), for example, claim that 'by eliciting a narrative structured according to the principles of free association ... we secure access to a person's concerns'. Occasional signals about the uncertainty of interview statements deviate from such self-confidence, but reservations about what interviews really say tend to disappear in the use of them to persuade the reader that here we have credible and convincing data supporting researchers' claims. Only to a modest extent have interview methodologists outside the localist camps begun 'to realize that we cannot lift the results of interviewing out of the contexts in which they were gathered and claim them as objective data with no strings attached' (Fontana & Frey, 2000: 663). But this emergent insight is mainly restricted to acknowledging this complication and to a general call for awareness and recognition; there are not many efforts to develop a theoretical framework to understand context issues. This book has aimed to do so and has proposed a rethink of what are conventionally seen as sources of bias for these to be minimized through various techniques and be viewed as key features of interviews calling for an ambitious theoretical understanding.

In this project I have to some extent drawn upon and developed the work of localist authors such as Potter and Wetherell and Silverman. They tend to emphasize close readings of language use in the micro-situation (conversations, chunks of text) and do not address the broader contextual issues affecting interviews, such as political motives and the role of discourse in a Foucauldian sense. A strict localist approach would undermine the options for studying meaning and experience as well as social practices beyond language use. So would a poststructuralist view on discourse, suggesting that texts construct and create effects rather than reveal meaning. The view proposed here then does not go as far as – or goes beyond, depending on how one sees it – localist or poststructuralist focus on detailed text or conversation analysis or deconstructions of discourse. The book differs from localist work in suggesting and indicating possible ways to check the dynamics undermining the interview as a knowledge producing activity and at least to some extent, under certain conditions, saving this project. It also differs by pointing at research problems bridging localist and conventional, broader concerns. Other differences concern ideas on different ways of using interpretive material, including downplaying its descriptive value and seeing it as inspiration for idea-generation or support in analysis.

Instead of strongly relying on researchers to optimize interviews as a technique or tool and/or to work hard in interview encounters in order to get interviewees to be honest, clear and consistent, the message expressed in the present book rather is that a lot of the hard work should be conducted at one's desk and that this is not primarily a matter of coding and processing data in an objective way. This view means that we should be skeptical but not dismissive of interview material, should not take it at face value and should avoid accepting it as a building block for knowledge that may be rationally dealt with through coding, etc. Instead, intensive interpretation about what interview statements may indicate and the mobilization of good reasons for how to use them are necessary. Fieldwork is of course important, but the complexities and pitfalls involved call for careful, on-going reflection and not just a well thought-out design and execution of this. There is thus a strong need to think through a) our basic theoretical stance on (metaphors of) interviews, b) the possible research tasks that we can expect to carry out in interviews, avoiding putting too heavy a burden on the meagre shoulders of the interviewer and the interviewee, and realizing that language cannot really mirror (complex) reality, and c) how we relate to empirical material emerging out of interviews, i.e. consider a variety of possible meanings in an open and (self-) critical way.

These considerations lead to a more modest, more reflexive approach to interviews than the dominating tool and pipeline version. Interviews cannot be reduced to simple (or even complicated) instruments – this metaphor for interviews is misleading if not challenged – but must be carefully considered also, but not necessarily exclusively, as complex social phenomena. In this book eight such conceptualizations have been suggested: as local accomplishment within a specific scene, perpetuating a storyline, identity work, a cultural script application, impression management, political action, construction work and a play of the powers of discourse. Some of these are based on localist thinking – in particular local accomplishment and script application – while most others draw upon other intellectual inspirations (identity theory, political theory, Foucauldian discourse theory, etc.).

In the book I have suggested four implications of new insights about the complexities of interviews and difficulties in knowing what goes on and thus the problems inherent in using them as pipelines to – or even as half-reliable indicators of – social facts and meanings.

1 *More thoughtful interventions when doing research work* It is very difficult for researchers to control the interview situation. It is far more complicated than a simuli-response model suggests. An interviewee may think quite differently about the purpose, what is relevant to talk about and how to understand the questions intended by the researcher. Some level of control (quality assessment) over what is happening and what informs the answers is necessary. Interventions such as presenting the project and researcher in different ways, introducing and steering away from various discourses, invoking different identities in different (or the same) interviews, etc. are not intended to make sure that the interviewee answers exactly as intended, but are aimed at giving the researcher a much better chance to understand what is happening in an interview. If one and the same theme is addressed through different entrances and leads to different interview talk, we can assume that the responses are less about a serious effort/ability to reflect reality out there or stable ideas about it, than about how local interaction, the use of vocabularies, various identity positions, etc. can trigger specific kinds of talk. If the talk remains fairly consistent despite variations in the various inputs and framing of the interview, then it seems more likely that one can use the interview material to move outside of the local situation and the self-referring quality of language use.

2 *Interpreting more carefully the meaning of interview material* It is important not to overestimate how much can actually be accomplished through more advanced interview tactics and practices. The perhaps most fundamental implication of the arguments and ideas of this book concern how researchers must think through what the empirical material is about and the sort of purposes it can be used for. This is very different from conventional approaches – here the value of interview data as indicating reality is assumed and the researcher builds on these to find out a deeper meaning or to discover patterns in the data. Grounded theorists, for example, would focus on the codification – not a critical interpretation and questioning – of the 'data' typically seen as robust ground for theory building (Charmaz, 2003). This tends to mean that researchers avoid assessing the value and possible uses of 'data' and rely on the seemingly fairly neutral position of taking its value more or less for granted.

Interview material produced in reflexively informed ways as suggested above may increase the chances of making well-informed judgments about the logics and mechanisms beyond the production of the interview talk. In most cases there will be a strong need to work through a number of alternative interpretations – alternative in relation to conventional concerns – and in many cases the alternative ones may carry equal or more weight than the conventional neo-positivist (instrument) or romanticist (human encounter) ones. And if it is equally plausible that the interview accounts are informed by following available social scripts or an accomplishment in the specific situation of a talk with a university person (or another interviewer) then it is difficult to use statements credibly for describing or interpreting the outer world or people's subjectivities. So reflexive methodology may make the use of interview material stronger and more rigorous, but in many cases the material may appear far too weak or ambiguous to be used for conventional purposes.

That means that researchers need either to drop or revise the original purpose or to work hard to find alternative ways to deliver, i.e. add supportive studies compensating for the limitations of the interview material. Participant observation is of course relevant here, although the limited scope of this needs to be recognized as we can't observe that much. One possibility is of course to add interviews with people who have another view on the research topic to that of the originally targeted group. If some people seem to be – or can be suspected of – employing conversational skills, expressing their idealized identity or acting politically, perhaps groups that know them but have a different take or interest on the subject matter can be approached. Instead of only or mainly interviewing managers about their leadership, perhaps their colleagues or subordinates can offer supplementary views. Talking to parents about their feelings about parenthood is perhaps ok, but if one can get the children's, relatives' or friends' views on these parents, one can better assess and possibly use the formers' accounts. The value of this should not be exaggerated – these others may not be all that well informed and may also be guided by other complex social factors, indicated by the eight metaphors – and of course this may often not be practically possible, but the point is that increased rigor calls for the scrutiny of the character of interview statements. The mobilization of support for why the reader should take interview talk seriously is crucial.

In many cases, such strengthening will not be possible and it would appear as arbitrary and speculative to move far beyond the interview talk as the empirical object of study. In this case, one option is (re-)define the research question so that it is possible to answer it with the empirical study.

3   *Development of new and innovate (and realistic) research questions*   Reflexive considerations should have drastic implications for which research task we embark on. Often methodological considerations are seen as secondary to the research question. You start with a purpose and then develop a method that seems to be appropriate to deliver the results. This is often naïve. Methodological awareness is necessary in order to formulate a good and answerable question. Considerations of the problems of going far beyond the interview situation mean that interview research should often avoid such speculative enterprises and more closely target what can actually be investigated. Finding creative and perhaps unexpected research questions that can be combined with a fairly rigorous approach is crucial here. This often means more 'discourse near' issues being targeted and/or situations not that dissimilar from the interview setting being focused on

for generalizations. If the interview is about impression management, an adaption to a set of norms, identity work, script-following, the subjectification to Big Discourse, etc., these are important phenomena and it would be possible to draw some conclusions about how these may also operate in contexts other than the interview. Here, one needs of course to take the variety of contexts into account and to use one's clinical judgements, plus the available empirical indicators on the range of contexts that the interview situation may say something about. Interview talk shows some resemblance with and some variation in relation to talk in other situations.

4   A final implication concerns implications for *going outside empirical claims*. Empirical materials like interviews are then, in many cases, not seen as allowing for strict description. The researcher may not be interested in or able to deliver the rigor needed to prove that s/he has studied more than just interview talk and can't make strong claims about the status and value of interviews. The empirical study can still be used for other, perhaps more modest, purposes, such as providing inspiration for new ideas, giving some uncertain clues about reality that may kick back at the researcher's bad ideas or being useful for illustrative purposes. Empirical work may simply be valuable in giving researchers some familiarity with the subject matter, making their theoretical reasoning more sensitive and empirically relevant. Given such a reduction in claims about the purposes for which interview material is used, issues around rigor and credibility become less of a problem. On the other hand, a soft and loose empirical study intended only to inspire or illustrate carries less weight, so researchers are probably wise to offer some really good ideas for theoretical contributions as a compensation for a 'weak' study. (Sometimes people will refer to their study as 'explorative' as an excuse for not delivering that much.)

One way of formulating this view could be to see empirical material (like interview statements) as a critical dialogue or analytical partner for the researcher rather than as the basic building block in research (Alvesson & Kärreman, 2011; Kreiner & Mouritsen, 2005). Interview talk is then appreciated for its capacity to generate new ideas or support interpretations of a phenomenon. If this is the purpose and overall understanding of the interview, it becomes less of an issue what guides the interviewee and puts the imprints on the interview. If the interview is seen as a 'mini-seminar' offering ideas and analytical help, then issues surrounding the validity of description (of practices, experiences, meanings or language uses) become less central.

A comment on voice and ethics

Before rounding off this book, a few words about the ethics of the research are called for. Most books and review articles on interviewing will contain a chapter or a section on this (e.g. Fontana & Frey, 2005;

Hollway & Jefferson, 2000, Chapter 5; Kvale, 1996, Chapter 6). Informed consent, confidentiality and truthful reporting are often key topics. Much of this seems self-evident, although in practice there may always be complications and dilemmas and life, including research life, is full of ethical compromise.[1] Of more interest to the present book are questions around voice and critical interpretation. One could say that researchers should have a lot of respect for those being studied and refrain from a critical assessment of their interview statements, or at least should be modest and careful when evaluating interviewee claims to tell the truth, as they see it – or at least report it. As Kvale says, an ethical issue involves 'how deeply and critically the interviews can be analyzed and of whether the subjects should have a say in how their statements are verified' (1996: 111). At one extreme, the researcher reduces him or herself to someone plying a microphone, reporting what people say without imposing anything or asking questions regarding what the statements are all about. At another extreme, the researcher intensively analyses and interprets interview material and may give this material a completely different meaning than that possibly intended by the interviewee. The interviewee's claim to tell a deep and authentic experience may, for example, be turned into an example of adapting to social standards for talking about a subject matter, thus doubting or at least not taking very seriously the claim to authenticity.

My position in this book comes closer to the second extreme, but I am eager to stress that great constraints and discipline are necessary here. Researchers should be careful when suggesting superior insights or truth-claims based on the privileged position they are in. I think it is normally good to avoid sticking to a tight theoretical framework – whether it is psychoanalysis, feminism, Foucauldian power-knowledge ideas or deconstruction – and applying it to empirical material, without being open to the possibilities of using the empirical material for other purposes. As Rorty (1989) says, one should work with an awareness that there may always be an alternative or even better vocabulary than the one favoured. Far too often, one reads empirical studies with predictable outcomes. So the issue of the researcher being in a strong asymmetrical relation to those being studied can to some extent be handled by efforts to doubt and challenge one's own favoured line of reasoning.

This does not directly solve or even fully address the issue of an assessment of the interview material. Most interviewees would probably assume that they are in the know, that they are truthful and they expect their statements to be respected, i.e. more or less accepted. The reflexive approach advocated here assumes that they may not know, may not be able to tell (that is, formulate specific insights into words), may be guided by other social logics and personal motives than truth-telling and that it would be naïve to take their statements more or less at face value.

Issues about power and elitism now enter the picture. A researcher applying a range of theories and considerations – in line with my eight metaphors framework – and potentially undermining the validity-claims and perhaps trustworthiness of those studied, clearly positions him or herself as, in some ways, superior to these people. Having access to, say, Foucauldian or identity theory means that one has an advantage in considering whether discourse or the struggle for identity construction informs interview talk. Use of researchers' richer access to interpretation possibilities is not unproblematic, as those interviewed are easily reduced to objects in the hands of a dissecting, analytical social science, which has the final say in terms of what is to be made of all this. This inclination to dissect and analyse is quite strong in localist positions such as conversation analysis and (some versions of) discourse analysis. When people's talk is put under the microscope and analytic framework, that talk appears very difficult from how it functions and is experienced in the social situations in which it was produced. Most people would probably feel alienated from what they have said in social settings if looking at a version of this as presented by conversation analysts, for example, and also feel that the transcript gives a rather strange, sterile and distorted representation of the interaction it claims to capture.

I don't think we can avoid the problem of representation being also a 'misrepresentation', where the voices of interviewees (or other participants in interactions) don't come out as they may have preferred. The task of social science is not simply to bring out the voices of people in the field; there are political parties, social movements, letters to the editor, journalists, fiction authors and others that are much better for such purposes. Researchers should take seriously the complexities of social life and these play a major role also in the production of interview processes.

Sometimes one can consider inviting those being studied to reflect and comment upon researchers' interpretations and text drafts. This can provide useful feedback (and a lot of complexities) but the final say on the interpretation and text is the responsibility of the researcher. On the whole, I think the approach suggested in this book can be used with an empathy for those being studied. That we relate their statements not only to the perhaps often very difficult task of reporting the truth (about reality out there or the experiences and meanings of those studied), but also to social conditions, interaction effects, difficulties to produce credible and coherent constructions, the impact of social norms and standards for talking about specific issues (we all feel the pressure of political correctness), etc., should not necessarily be seen as downgrading the views of the interviewee. Acknowledging the difficulties inherent in making the interview situation work as a pipeline for accessing facts or subjectivities and recognizing the range of possible motives for talk may insult strong advocates of an interview society and those reproducing dominant ideology in qualitative research, both researchers and interviewees. But I do think that a more 'realistic' appreciation of the situation and an increased ability and interest in critically examining what goes on are in the interests of most people and that this should be the overall 'ethical principle'.

This is not, of course, an excuse for simply running down the claims for the interviews without good reasons and careful reflection. Researchers need to consider the risks of being arrogant or taking an ungrounded superior position. Critical reflection does not have to involve an emphasis on a strong social distance, even though some element (stage) of this is useful, indeed necessary, in parts of the research process. Empathy and understanding can and should also guide interpretation and the writing of 'problematic' aspects like conformism and political action in interviews. The reflexive author can easily point to similar tendencies in his/her own life and work, including in the texts produced, where knowledge claims sometimes reflect less what was studied than an adaption to what was needed to get published and impress one's colleagues. (I have already pointed at the tendency of academics to move from reflexivity to a simple reporting of supportive interviews treated as facts, in order to adapt to a journal format and the perceived expectations of reviewers and readers in order to be published and read.) Combinations of a set of considerations should then make the use of critical reflexivity advocated here less of a moral dilemma than what some researchers being (too) close to and sympathetic to those studied may perhaps feel. Note that I am saying 'less of' a moral dilemma. We can't avoid moral dilemmas in life in general and research is no exception. Following formalized ethical rules is seldom a safe way to be ethical; it easily leads to rule-following and a limited interest in wider ethical reflection. Formal rules are seldom that helpful – they tend to be vague or rigid – and people may have an excuse for not thinking about ethics in those areas not covered by the rules. Rule-following means that 'ethics' can be ticked off – a form of ethical closure (Kärreman & Alvesson, 2010). But as said, I don't think that taking full responsibility for a critical interpretation of interview statements means a stronger moral burden than a naïve belief in the statements being more or less uncritically reproduced as valuable data.

Final words

I have no doubt that many readers of this book, in particular more experienced ones, would feel that they, as good researchers, are already sensitive to and can grasp – and perhaps even deal with – some of the issues addressed in the eight metaphors. I do suspect however that it is mainly or only the more obvious examples of superficial talk, politically motivated acts or over-adaptation to the researcher that would be detected. The general norm in interview-based research seems to be to have faith in the 'data' and then to not question it very much but, as in grounded theory, to spend most energy with the sorting and codification of the transcribed interview material. It is then framed and (selectively) presented as authoritative material indicating facts or meanings. Any deeper understanding or problematization of subject matters in line with the view suggested here seems to be quite uncommon. It is rare, particularly in reported interview-based studies, to find examples of a willingness and capacity to explore fully the possibility that the interview may not work as a tool or human encounter effectively guided by researchers' interest in tapping interviewees for knowledge. (Some specialized discourse and conversation analysis plus some authors on poststructuralism – what I have in this book summarized as localism – are important exceptions here.) A more profound awareness of the themes indicated by my eight metaphors is needed. By suggesting that these should be taken seriously and seen as competing forces to truth- or experience-telling, a more ambitious level of methodological reflexivity is suggested. I am aware that this also suggests some added difficulties for interview researchers, but this can't be helped.

That I am targeting interviews in this book and delivering a range of critical views on what I see as mainstream approaches (tool and human encounter views) does not mean that other methods and techniques are better or easier to work with. There are considerable difficulties also with ethnographies, as witnessed in a wealth of writings on the subject (Marcus & Fisher, 1986; Van Maanen, 1995). A lot of the critique that I raise is also relevant for appreciating questionnaires and here one has good reason to apply the whip even more fiercely. One may often ask whether questionnaires say that much more than capturing how some people put x's in squares when they fill in a form. But as the topic of this book is interviews, especially qualitative (loosely structured) ones, I have refrained from commenting in any depth on other approaches. The reader should not have too much difficulty in drawing out implications for other practices in social and behavioural science than interviews.

A theoretical understanding of the research interview means conceptualizing what goes on in a situation and how its outcomes can be understood. It means a 'thicker' understanding than that provided by the interview-as-technique-for-getting-data or the interview-as-human-encounter-leading-to-an-in-depth-shared-understanding. As emphasized throughout this book, the multiple layers of meaning involved in interview work, and the contingencies of the performances of the interviewee, need to be appreciated. In our 'interview society', we have institutionalized the interview; many people have picked up the clues and can perform interviews without too much friction and convey the impression of being honest, sincere, open and trustworthy. We should not fall into the trap of necessarily believing that these impressions say that much. They may be sufficient for the success of Dr Phil or Oprah and other talk show hosts celebrating the expression of intimacy in front of millions of viewers, as well as for journalists producing news in the form of interviews with politicians, executives and media celebrities, but as social scientists we must aim for considerably higher standards.

We have three major basic elements calling for deep reflection: i) the social scene (involving the interviewer, but also the physical setting and general framing of the situation); ii) the individual (interviewee) subject targeted as constituted in terms of (the interaction of) identity, impression regulation, sense making and politics, and with a motive-orientation that is crucial for the accounts produced; and iii) the double-edged nature of language: speaking behind and through the subject, constituting him/her, and forward-oriented, evoking effects on listeners. Tying this together is not easy. It is not necessarily productive either. The scene, the subject and the language offer different entrances and foci for understanding what goes on in an interview. In this book, deep thinking about how we conceptualize and use interviews is encouraged through the proposal of addressing the level of the metaphor behind surface practice and technique. The advantage of conceptualizing something in terms of metaphors is that it avoids a categorical position on the subject matter. It challenges and inspires rather than suggests a firm position. It opens up our ways of looking at the interview from prematurely and unreflectively seeing it as a researcher-controlled tool or as a human encounter for the co-production of knowledge in favour of critical inter-pretations of specific interview situations and accounts. Instead of a method-technical focus, the interview is placed in an epistemological-theoretical-methodological context. This is much needed.

A set of metaphors can be put together as an interpretive repertoire guided by a metatheoretical framework in which: i) the interview situation is seen as a socially, linguistically and subjectively rich and complex situation, open in terms of knowledge-producing potential in relationship to other features; ii) the interview is seen as possible to use for a variety of research purposes; iii) but where an assessment of the usefulness of the material and a strengthening of the kind of approach taken call for multi-angled interpretation and a preparedness to reconsider favoured lines of inquiry in light of alternative ones. Research interviews call for a wide set of considerations depending on one's purpose and also on how specific examples empirically unfold. Key aspects are a problematizing attitude and a willingness to engage with theoretically informed interpretations about the interview situation and the various 'logics' behind interview statements. The theoretical framework and vocabulary suggested here are intended to support the critical judgement that must be viewed as the cornerstone in research. The conflict between these key elements in reflexive research and the traditional means of suppressing ambiguity and accomplishing pseudo-rationality – through data management and technical rules – should not be underestimated.

Note

1 For example, preserving anonymity may call for some camouflaging of the sample, i.e. not just giving those studied fictive names, but also, at least on sensitive issues, giving some misleading information, which then may violate the ideal of being truthful in the report. Another example concerns how people's voices are represented, which by necessity always needs to be done in a partial way and sometimes with a concern for how socially vulnerable groups may appear (Fine et al., 2000). And in order to present something 'interesting' representations will tend to be highly selective and a lot of complexity and nuance will need to be bypassed. Different ethical (and other) ideals can often contradict each other and compromises are unavoidable.

REFERENCES

Acker, J., Barry, K. and Esseveld, J. (1991) 'Objectivity and truth: problems in doing feminist research', in M. Fonow and J. Cook (eds), *Beyond Methodology: Feminist Scholarship as Lived Research*. Bloomington: Indiana University Press.

Alvesson, M. (1994) 'Talking in organizations: managing identity and impressions in an advertising agency', *Organization Studies*, 15: 535–563.

Alvesson, M. (1995) *Management of Knowledge-Intensive Companies*. Berlin/New York: de Gruyter.

Alvesson, M. (2002) *Postmodernism and Social Research*. Buckingham: Open University Press.

Alvesson, M. (2006) *Tomhetens triumf. Grandiositet, illusionsnummer och nollsummespel*. Stockholm: Atlas.

Alvesson, M. (2010) 'Self-doubters, strugglers, story-tellers, surfers and others: images of self-identity in organization studies', *Human Relations*, 63(2): 193–227.

Alvesson, M. (2011) 'The leader as saint', in M. Alvesson and A. Spicer (eds), *Metaphors we Lead by: Understanding Leadership in the Real World*. London: Routledge.

Alvesson, M. and Billing, Y.D. (2009) *Understanding Gender and Organization* (2nd edn). London: SAGE.

Alvesson, M. and Deetz, S. (2000) *Doing Critical Management Research*. London: SAGE.

Alvesson, M., Hardy, C. and Harley, B. (2008) 'Reflecting on reflexivity: reappraising reflexive practice in organisation and management theory', *Journal of Management Studies*, 45 (3): 480–501.

Alvesson, M. and Kärreman, D. (2000a) 'Taking the linguistic turn in organizational research: challenges, responses, consequences', *Journal of Applied Behavioural Science*, 36: 136–158.

Alvesson, M. and Kärreman, D. (2000b) 'Varieties of discourse: on the study of organizations through discourse analysis', *Human Relations*, 53 (9): 1125–1149.

Alvesson, M. and Kärreman, D. (2007) 'Unraveling HRM: identity, ceremony and control in a management consultancy firm', *Organization Science*, 18 (4): 711–723.

Alvesson, M. and Kärreman, D. (2011) *Constructing Mystery*. London: SAGE.

Alvesson, M. and Sköldberg, K. (2009) *Reflexive Methodology* (2nd edn). London: SAGE.

Alvesson, M. and Sveningsson, S. (2003) 'The good visions, the bad micro-management and the ugly ambiguity: contradictions of (non-) leadership in a knowledge-intensive company', *Organization Studies*, 24 (6): 961–988.

Archer, M. (1998) 'Introduction: realism in the social sciences', in M. Archer, R. Bhaskar, A. Collier, T. Lawson and A. Norrie (eds), *Critical Realism: Essential Reading*. London: Routledge.

Asplund, J. (1970) *Om undran inför samhället*. Lund: Argos.

Astley, G. (1985) 'Administrative science as socially constructed truth', *Administrative Science Quarterly*, 30: 497–513.

Baker, C. (1997) 'Membership categorizations and interview accounts', in D. Silverman (ed.), *Qualitative Research*. London: SAGE.

Baker, C. (2003) 'Ethnomethodological analysis of interviews', in J. Holstein and J. Gubrium (eds), *Inside Interviewing*. Thousand Oaks, CA: SAGE.

Barker, J. (1993) 'Tightening the iron cage: concertive control in self-managing teams', *Administrative Science Quarterly*, 38: 408–437.

Bhaskar, R. (1998) 'General introduction', in M. Archer et al. (eds), *Critical Realism*. London: Routledge.

Boje, D. (1991) 'The story-telling organization: a study of story performance in an office-supply firm', *Administrative Science Quarterly*, 36: 106–126.

Brewer, J. (2000) *Ethnography*. Buckingham: Open University Press.

Briggs, C. (2003) 'Interviewing, power/knowledge and social inequality', in J. Holstein and J. Gubrium (eds), *Inside Interviewing*. Thousand Oaks, CA: SAGE.

Brown, R.H. (1976) 'Social theory as metaphor', *Theory and Society*, 3: 169–197.

Brown, R.H. (1977) *A Poetic for Sociology*. Chicago: University of Chicago Press.

Brown, R.H. (1990) 'Rhetoric, textuality, and the postmodern turn in sociological theory', *Sociological Theory*, 8: 188–197.

Bryman, A. et al. (1988) 'Qualitative research and the study of leadership', *Human Relations*, 41 (1): 13–30.

Charmaz, K. (2003) 'Qualitative interviewing and grounded theory analysis', in J. Holstein and J. Gubrium (eds), *Inside Interviewing*. Thousand Oaks, CA: SAGE.

Cicourel, A. (1964) *Method and Measurement in Sociology*. New York: Free.

Clifford, J. (1986) 'Introduction: partial truths', in J. Clifford and G.E. Marcus (eds), *Writing Culture: The Poetics and Politics of Ethnography*. Berkeley: University of California Press.

Collinson, D. (1992) 'Researching recruitment: qualitative methods and sex discrimination', in R. Burgess (ed.), *Studies in Qualitative Methodology Vol. 3*. Greenwich, CT: JAI.

Cornelissen, J. and Kafauros, M. (2008) 'The emergent organization: primary and complex metaphors in theorizing about organizations', *Organization Studies*, 29 (7): 957–977.

Covaleski, M. et al. (1998) 'The calculated and the avowed: techniques of discipline and struggles over identity in Big Six public accounting firms', *Administrative Science Quarterly*, 43: 293–327.

Czarniawska-Joerges, B. (1992) *Exploring Complex Organizations*. Newbury Park, CA: SAGE.

Deetz, S. (1992) *Democracy in the Age of Corporate Colonization: Developments in Communication and the Politics of Everyday Life*. Albany: State University of New York Press.

Delanty, G. (2005) *Social Science* (2nd edn). Buckingham: Open University Press.

Denzin, N. (1994) 'The art and politics of interpretation', in N. Denzin and Y. Lincoln (eds), *Handbook of Qualitative Research*. Thousand Oaks, CA: SAGE.

Denzin, N. (1997) *Interpretive Ethnography*. Thousand Oaks, CA: SAGE.

Denzin, N. and Lincoln, Y. (1994) 'Introduction: entering the field of qualitative research', in N. Denzin and Y. Lincoln (eds), *Handbook of Qualitative Research*. Thousand Oaks, CA: SAGE.

Denzin, N. and Lincoln, Y. (2005) 'Introduction: the discipline and practice of qualitative research', in N. Denzin and Y. Lincoln (eds), *Handbook of Qualitative Research* (3rd edn). Thousand Oaks, CA: SAGE.

DeVault, M. (1990) 'Talking and listening from women's standpoint: feminist strategies for interviewing and analysis', *Social Problems,* 37: 96–116.

Dingwall, R. (1997) 'Accounts, interviews and observations', in G. Miller and R. Dingwall (eds), *Context & Method in Qualitative Research*. London: SAGE.

Eagly, A. and Carli, L. (2007) 'Women and the labyrinth of leadership', *Harvard Business Review*, Sept: 62–71.

Easterby-Smith, M., Thorpe, R. and Lowe, A. (1991) *Management Research: An Introduction*. London: SAGE.

Eisenhardt, K. (1989) 'Building theories from case study research', *Academy of Management Review*, 14: 532–550.

Ellis, C. et al. (1997) 'Interactive interviewing', in R. Hertz (ed.), *Reflexivity and Voice*. Thousand Oaks, CA: SAGE.

Ely, R. (1995) 'The power in demography: women's social constructions of gender identity at work', *Academy of Management Journal*, 38: 589–634.

Essers, C. and Benschop, Y. (2007) 'Enterprising identities: female entrepreneurs of Turkish or Moroccan origin in the Netherlands', *Organization Studies*, 28 (1): 49–69.

Fangen, K. (2007) 'Breaking up the different constituting parts of ethnicity: the case of young Somalis in Norway', *Acta Sociologica*, 50 (4): 401–414.

Fine, M. et al. (2000) 'For whom? Qualitative research, representations and social responsibilities', in N. Denzin and Y. Lincoln (eds), *Handbook of Qualitative Research* (2nd edn). Thousand Oaks, CA: SAGE.

Fontana, A. and Frey, J. (1994) 'Interviewing: the art of science', in N. Denzin and Y. Lincoln (eds), *Handbook of Qualitative Research*. Thousand Oaks, CA: SAGE.

Fontana, A. and Frey, J. (2000) 'The interview: from structured questions to negotiated text', in N. Denzin and Y. Lincoln (eds), *Handbook of Qualitative Research* (2nd edn). Thousand Oaks, CA: SAGE.

Fontana, A. and Frey, J. (2005) 'The interview: from neutral stance to political involvement', in N. Denzin and Y. Lincoln (eds), *Handbook of Qualitative Research* (3rd edn). Thousand Oaks, CA: SAGE.

Foucault, M. (1980) *Power/Knowledge*. New York: Pantheon.

Gabriel, Y. and Lang, T. (1995) *The Unmanageable Consumer*. London: SAGE.

Geertz, C. (1983) *Local Knowledge*. New York: Basic.

Gergen, K. and Gergen, M. (1991) 'Toward reflexive methodologies', in F. Steier (ed.), *Research and Reflexivity*. London: SAGE.

Glaser, B.G. and Strauss, A.L. (1967) *The Discovery of Grounded Theory: Strategies for Qualitative Research*. Chicago, IL: Aldine.

Grant, D. and Oswick, C. (eds) (1996) *Metaphor and Organization*. London: SAGE.

Grant, D. et al. (eds) (1998) *Discourse and Organization*. London: SAGE.

Grey, C. (1994) 'Career as a project of the self and labour process discipline', *Sociology*, 28: 479–497.

Guba, E. and Lincoln, Y. (1994) 'Competing paradigms in qualitative research', in N.K. Denzin and Y.S. Lincoln (eds), *Handbook of Qualitative Research*. Thousand Oaks, CA: SAGE.

Hammersley, M. and Atkinson, P. (1994) 'Ethnography and participant observation', in N. Denzin and Y. Lincoln (eds), *Handbook of Qualitative Research*. Thousand Oaks, CA: SAGE.

Hertz, R. (1997) 'Introduction: reflexivity and voice', in R. Hertz (ed.), *Reflexivity and Voice*. Thousand Oaks: SAGE.

Hollway, W. (1984) 'Fitting work: psychological assessment in organizations', in J. Henriques, W. Hallway, C. Urwin, C. Venn and V. Walkerdine (eds), *Changing the Subject*. New York: Methuen.

Hollway, W. (1989) *Subjectivity and Method in Psychology*. London: SAGE.

Hollway, W. and Jefferson, T. (2000) *Doing Qualitative Research Differently*. London: SAGE.

Holstein, J.A. and Gubrium, J. (1997) 'Active interviewing', in D. Silverman (ed.), *Qualitative Research*. London: SAGE.

Holstein, J.A. and Gubrium, J. (2003a) 'Inside interviewing: new lenses, new concerns', in J. Holstein and J. Gubrium (eds), *Inside Interviewing*. Thousand Oaks, CA: SAGE.

Holstein, J.A. and Gubrium, J. (eds) (2003b) *Inside Interviewing*. Thousand Oaks, CA: SAGE.

Inns, D. and Jones, P. (1996) 'Metaphor in organization theory: following in the footstep of the poet', in D. Grant and C. Oswick (eds), *Metaphor and Organizations*. London: SAGE.

Jackall, R. (1988) *Moral Mazes: The World of Corporate Managers*. Oxford: Oxford University Press.

Jorgenson, J. (1991) 'Co-constructing the interviewer/Co-constructing "family"', in F. Steier (ed.), *Research and Reflexivity*. London: SAGE.

Kärreman, D. and Alvesson, M. (2009) 'Resisting resistance: on counter-resistance, control and compliance in a consultancy firm', *Human Relations*, 62 (8): 1115–1144.

Kärreman, D. and Alvesson, M. (2010) 'Ethical closure in organizational settings – the case of media organizations', in S. Muhr, B.M. Sørensen and S. Vallentin (eds), *Ethics and Organizational Practice – Questioning the Moral Foundations of Management*. Cheltenham: Edward Elgar.

Kilduff, M. and Mehra, A. (1997) 'Postmodernism and organizational research', *Academy of Management Review*, 22: 453–481.

Kreiner, K. and Mouritsen, J. (2005) 'The analytic interview', in S. Tengblad et al. (eds), *The Art of Science*. Malmö: Liber.

Kvale, S. (1996) *Inter-viewing*. London: SAGE.

Lakoff, G. and Johnson, M. (1980) *Metaphors We Live By*. Chicago: University of Chicago Press.

Lee, N. and Hassard, J. (1999) 'Organization unbound: actor-network theory, research strategy and institutional flexibility', *Organization*, 6 (3): 391–404.

Lidström-Widell, G. (1995) *Organisationsbilder* [Organizational images]. PhD thesis, Gothenburg, BAS.

Lynch, M. (2000) 'Against reflexivity as an academic virtue and source of privileged knowledge', *Theory, Culture, & Society*, 17: 26–54.

Marcus, G. and Fischer, M. (1986) *Anthropology as Cultural Critique*. Chicago: University of Chicago Press.

Martin, J. (1992) *The Culture of Organizations: Three Perspectives*. New York: Oxford University Press.

Martin, J. et al. (1983) 'The uniqueness paradox in organizational stories', *Administrative Science Quarterly*, 28: 438–453.

Martin, J. et al. (1998) 'An alternative to bureaucratic impersonality and emotional labour: bounded emotionality at the Body Shop', *Administrative Science Quarterly*, 43: 429–469.

Miller, J. and Glassner, B. (1997) 'The "inside" and the "outside": finding realities in interviews', in D. Silverman (ed.), *Qualitative Research*. London: SAGE.

Mills, C.W. (1940) 'Situated actions and vocabularies of motives', *American Sociological Review*, 5: 904–913.

Morgan, G. (1980) 'Paradigms, metaphors and puzzle solving in organization theory', *Administrative Science Quarterly*, 25: 605–622.

Morgan, G. (ed.) (1983) *Beyond Method*. Newbury Park, CA: SAGE.

Morgan, G. (1986) *Images of Organization*. Newbury Park, CA: SAGE.

Morgan, G. (1996) 'An afterword: is there anything more to be said about metaphors?', in D. Grant and C. Oswick (eds), *Metaphor and Organization*. London: SAGE.

Morgan, G. (1997) *Images of Organization* (2nd edn). Thousand Oaks, CA: SAGE.

Newton, T. (1996) 'Agency and discourse: recruiting consultants in a life insurance company', *Sociology*, 30 (4): 717–739.

Newton, T. (1998) 'Theorizing subjectivity in organizations: the failure of Foucauldian studies?', *Organization Studies*, 19: 415–448.

Olesen, V. (2000) 'Feminism and qualitative research at and into the millennium', in N. Denzin and Y. Lincoln (eds), *Handbook of Qualitative Research* (2nd edn). Thousand Oaks, CA: SAGE.

Parker, M. (2000) *Organizational Culture and Identity*. London: SAGE.

Pfeffer, J. (1981) *Power in Organizations*. Boston, MA: Pitman.

Pinder, C. and Bourgeois, V. (1982) 'Controlling tropes in administrative science', *Administrative Science Quarterly*, 27: 641–652.

Potter, J. (1996) *Representing Reality*. London: SAGE.

Potter, J. (1997) 'Discourse analysis as a way of analysing naturally occurring talk', in D. Silverman (ed.), *Qualitative Research*. London: SAGE.

Potter, J. and Wetherell, M. (1987) *Discourse and Social Psychology: Beyond Attitudes and Behaviour*. London: SAGE.

Pratt, M. (2008) 'Fitting oral pegs into rounded holes: tensions in evaluating and publishing qualitative research in top-tier North American journals', *Organizational Research Methods*, 11: 481–509.

Prior, L. (1997) 'Following in Foucault's footstep: text and context in qualitative research', in D. Silverman (ed.), *Qualitative Research*. London: SAGE.

Reed, M. (1990) 'From paradigms to images: the paradigm warrior turns post-modern guru', *Personnel Review*, 19 (3): 35–40.

Reinharz, S. (1997) 'Who am I? The need for a variety of selves in fieldwork', in R. Hertz (ed.), *Reflexivity and Voice*. Thousand Oaks, CA: SAGE.

Reinharz, S. and Chase, S. (2003) 'Interviewing women', in J. Holstein and J. Gubrium (eds), *Inside Interviewing*. Thousand Oaks, CA: SAGE.

Richardson, L. (2000) 'Writing: a method of inquiry', in N. Denzin and Y. Lincoln (eds), *Handbook of Qualitative Research* (2nd edn). Thousand Oaks, CA: SAGE.

Ricoeur, P. (1978) 'Metaphor and the main problem of hermeneutics', in C.E. Reagan and D. Stewart (eds), *The Philosophy of Paul Ricoeur*. Boston, MA: Beacon.

Riessman, C. (2003) 'Analysis of personal narratives', in J. Holstein and J. Gubrium (eds), *Inside Interviewing*. Thousand Oaks, CA: SAGE.

Rorty, R. (1989) *Contingency, Irony and Solidarity*. Cambridge: Cambridge University Press.

Rosen, M. (1991) 'Coming to terms with the field: understanding and doing organizational ethnography', *Journal of Management Studies*, 28: 1–24.

Rosenau, P.M. (1992) *Post-modernism and the Social Sciences: Insights, Inroads, and Intrusions*. Princeton: Princeton University Press.

Scheurich, J. (1997) *Research Methods in the Postmodern*. London: Falmer.

Schneider, B. (2000) 'Managers as evaluators: invoking objectivity to achieve objectives', *Journal of Applied Behavioural Science*, 36: 159–173.

Schön, D. (1979) 'Generative metaphor: a perspective on problem-setting in social policy', in A. Ortony (ed.), *Metaphor*. Cambridge: Cambridge University Press.

Schwalbe, M. and Wolkomir, M. (2003) 'Interviewing men', in J. Holstein and J. Gubrium (eds), *Inside Interviewing*. Thousand Oaks, CA: SAGE.

Sennett, R. (1977) *The Fall of Public Man*. New York: Vintage.

Sennett, R. (1980) *Authority*. New York: Vintage.

Silverman, D. (1985) *Qualitative Methodology & Sociology*. Aldershot: Gower.

Silverman, D. (1993) *Interpreting Qualitative Data*. London: SAGE.

Silverman, D. (2006) *Interpreting Qualitative Data* (3rd edn). London: SAGE.

Skeggs, B. (1994) 'Situating the production of feminist ethnography', in M. Maynard and J. Purvis (eds), *Researching Women's Lives from a Feminist Perspective*. London: Taylor & Francis.

Skeggs, B. (1997) *Formations of Class and Gender*. London: SAGE.

Steier, F. (ed.) (1991) *Research and Reflexivity*. London: SAGE.

Thomas, J. (1993) *Doing Critical Ethnography*. Newbury Park, CA: SAGE.

Thomas, R. and Davies, A. (2005) 'Theorising the micro-politics of resistance: discourses of change and professional identities in the UK Public Services', *Organization studies*, 26 (5): 683–706.

Tinker, T. (1986) 'Metaphor or reification: are radical humanists really libertarian anarchists?', *Journal of Management Studies*, 25: 363–384.

Tsoukas, H. (1991) 'The missing link: a transformational view of metaphors in organizational science', *Academy of Management Review*, 16: 566–585.

Ulver-Sneistrup, S. (2008) *Status Spotting: A Consumer Cultural Exploration into Ordinary Status Consumption of 'Home' and Home Aesthetics*. Lund Studies in Economics and Management 102. Lund: Lund Business Press.

Van Maanen, J. (1988) *Tales of the Field*. Chicago: University of Chicago Press.

Van Maanen, J. (ed.) (1995) *Representation in Ethnography*. Thousand Oaks, CA: SAGE.

von Glasersfeld, E. (1991) 'Knowing without metaphysics: aspects of the radical constructivist position', in F. Steier (ed.), *Research and Reflexivity*. London: SAGE.

Watson, T. (1994) *In Search of Management*. London: Routledge.

Weedon, C. (1987) *Feminist Practice and Poststructuralist Theory*. Oxford: Blackwell.

Whyte, W.F. (1960) 'Interviewing in field research', in R. Burgess (ed.), *Field Research*. London: Routledge.

Woolgar, S. (1983) 'Irony in the social studies of science', in K. Knorr-Cetina and M. Mulkay (eds), *Science Observed: Perspectives in the Social Study of Science*. London: SAGE.

Wray-Bliss, E. (2002) 'Abstract ethics, embodied ethics: the strange marriage of Foucault and positivism in labour process theory', *Organization*, 9 (1): 5–39.

SUBJECT INDEX

anti-positivism 37

categories 10, 49, 109
class 31
cognitive 63, 66, 72, 76, 84
conceptualizations 6, 8, 17, 24,
    65, 131
    re- 131
construction 36, 39, 70, 90, 99,
    110, 138
    work, interview as 95–7
conventions 3, 37, 80, 87–8, 129
conversation 7
    analysis 20
    skills 40, 145
cooperation 34
critical
    realism 5
    theory 70, 109
cultural script application, interview
    as 88–90

data 1–2, 39, 60, 75, 144, 150
    collection 54, 61, 68–9
    management 59, 73
    objective 65
discourse 1, 4, 51, 72, 98, 115, 132
    analysis 20
    metaphor 99
    power 99
D-reflexivity 108–10

emotionalism 11, 14, 20
epistemology 112–13, 152
empiricism 5, 59
establishing and perpetuating a story-
    line, interview as 82–4, 143
ethics 37, 146, 149

Foucaldian 37–8, 99, 109–10, 148
framework 45, 99, 105, 111–12, 152

grounded theory 1, 59, 69, 144, 150

high-brow methodology 5
hyper-romanticism 15, 20

identity 99
    work, interviews as 84–7, 91
image 6, 16, 29, 64, 68, 72, 92
    self 72, 86, 95, 125
impression management, interview as
    3, 90–1, 146
incongruence 10, 3
informant 29, 50–1, 72, 95, 114, 137
    key 13, 50–1, 53
interaction 11, 18, 54, 63
    interview 17
    social 80
interactive rationalism 11–13, 41
interpretation 40, 46, 120, 131
    work 60
interpretive 1, 102, 152
interventions 15, 123, 144
interview
    as an instrument 7
    research 11, 24, 103
    situation 32–3, 80–2
    society 3, 99
    standards 4
interview, types of
    group 9
    semi-structured 9, 53
    single 9, 118
    structured 9
    unstructured 9
interviewee 4, 81–3, 86, 92, 113

leadership 30, 85
lines of interpretation 7–8, 74, 106, 110–11, 131
local accomplishment, interview as 80–2, 143
localism 7, 19–24, 39–41, 142
low-brow method 5

macro
  cultural 36
  forces 34
masculinity 72, 87
meaning 12, 27, 40, 62–4, 72, 103, 144, 151
men 10, 72, 87
  interviewing 16
methodological
  individualism 4
  practice 2
micro 34
metaphor 6, 8, 41, 75–8, 100–1, 112
moral storytelling, interview as 90–2
marratives 23, 35, 71

neo-positivism 11, 39, 52, 80
non-descriptive purposes 123, 139
novel research question 8, 131

objective 12, 131
  reality 65
ontological 19, 114–15

perspective-shifting 7
political 29, 37, 92–5
  action, interview as 92–5
  metaphor 107
positivism 2
postmodernism 20, 109
poststructuralism 5, 37, 98
power 15, 99, 109–10, 148
  of discourse 98–9
  relations 10, 36, 38

practice 31, 54, 60, 122–5
practical aspects on interviews 44
pragmatism 7, 107
pre-understanding 1, 127

qualitative research 52, 58, 83
quantitative research 3, 12
quality 50, 116, 117
questionnaire 38, 54, 71
  research 2, 52

rational interactionism 38
reflexive pragmatism 6, 105, 108, 120
reflexive 37, 66, 106, 107, 120
  approach 4, 5, 106, 111
  practices 108
R-reflexivity 110
representation 1, 38, 76, 98, 148
representativeness 49
researcher-self 106
research questions 6, 8, 47, 114, 122, 131–2, 135, 145
respondents 12–15, 24, 29
rigor 3, 8, 65, 123, 131–2, 139
romanticism 7, 13, 52, 86, 92, 98

script 88, 96, 125
  application 143
self-examination 106
structure 9, 52
subjectivity 33, 98

tape-recorder, use of 44, 55–7
techniques 13, 125, 131, 142
technical aspects on interviews 43–6, 57
transcription of interviews 58
truth 1, 86

woman 16, 85, 94
  voice 51, 82, 147

AUTHOR INDEX

Research Methods Books from SAGE